Relish
COTSWOLDS &
OXFORDSHIRE

Original recipes from the Cotswolds and
Oxfordshire's finest chefs and restaurants.
Introduction by Chef Gary Jones, Le Manoir

First Published 2013
By Relish Publications
Shield Green Farm, Tritlington,
Northumberland, NE61 3DX.

ISBN: 978-0-9575370-1-9

Publisher: Duncan L Peters
General Manager: Teresa Peters
Design: Vicki Brown
Editorial Consultant: Paul Robertson
Published in association with
www.Gourmet-Lifestyle.co.uk
Sales and content: James Day,
www.leisuremarketingltd.co.uk
Additional content and photography: Andrew Richardson
Photography: Mark Green, www.talkingpictures.co.uk

Front cover photograph by Mark Green

Printed By: Balto Print Ltd, Stratford,
London E15 2TF.

Relish
PUBLICATIONS

THE HEART OF ENGLAND'S FINEST WITH GOURMET-LIFESTYLE

Relish is proud to be in partnership with Gourmet-lifestyle offering exclusive access
to many of the finest chefs, restaurants and their hotels across the region.
Membership entitles you to exclusive offers and unique gourmet-lifestyle experiences
in many of the venues featured in this book and in the Relish Midlands cookbook.

TASTY MEMBERSHIP TRIAL

As the proud owner of a Relish cookbook, you are entitled to three months free trial of the Gourmet-Life
Lifestyle Dining Club. Simply visit the link below and complete your application online to enjoy the exclusive
offers from some of these stunning venues.

JOIN TODAY - www.gourmet-life.co.uk/relish-cook-book www.twitter.com/gourmet_life

004
CONTENTS

DESSERTS

RESTAURANTS

006
CONTENTS

DESSERTS

RESTAURANTS

INTRODUCTION WITH CHEF GARY JONES

Food has been the biggest passion of my life. I have worked with some of the world's greatest chefs and in some of the best known kitchens of all. Holding the post of head chef at Le Manoir aux Quat'Saisons has been a dream come true. It's my honour that Monsieur Raymond Blanc has entrusted me with that post for the past decade - I am privileged indeed.

I first came to Le Manoir many years ago. It was a very different place back then. At that time, we were part owned by Richard Branson and we had 13 chefs in the main kitchen. Now there are around 40.

I didn't stay. Instead, I went to Necker Island to work for Richard, before eventually returning to the UK. I asked myself what I wanted and it was a Michelin star. I worked at Homewood Park, then Waldo's at the Cliveden and then the telephone rang. It was Raymond Blanc. He wanted me to come to dinner and that was that.

Persuasive as Monsieur Blanc is, he didn't have to work too hard to convince me to return. I'd achieved a Michelin star at Waldo's and returning to Le Manoir was what I wanted the most.

Our kitchen is an exceptional place in which to work. We have two Michelin stars and our restaurant is one of the best and most respected in the world.

It has been a privilege to work with Monsieur Blanc. His life-long love affair with food was sparked by Maman Blanc's lovingly-created family meals. She focused on fresh, local, seasonal flavours - an ethos that remains with us today.

Monsieur Blanc opened his first restaurant in Oxford in 1977, Les Quat'Saisons, and it won the Egon Ronay Restaurant of the Year. Seven years later, he fulfilled his dream of opening a hotel and restaurant that combined an elegant environment with gastronomic excellence - Le Manoir aux Quat'Saisons.

I am proud to be part of it. Our grounds are thrilling because they have an extensive vegetable and herb garden. That means we are able to select the freshest, seasonal produce and bring it to the table each day. We have an ethical approach to cooking and we respect the environment.

One of the greatest joys of working at Le Manoir aux Quat'Saisons has been the opportunity to work with new talent. We have worked with a great many chefs and sommeliers, waiters and waitresses over the years. Many have gone on to open their own restaurants. A great number have achieved Michelin stars - some appearing alongside us in this book.

There is nothing more remarkable than seeing young people who apply themselves earn their reward through hard work. Young chefs are the future talents of tomorrow. We are very proud of our protégés.

Relish Oxfordshire and Cotswolds brings together some of the most talented chefs from this region. It shines the spotlight on the exceptional ways in which fresh, seasonal, local ingredients are put to good use. It gives you a taste of the food that makes this region so special. I hope that you enjoy it and that you continue to support our region's great restaurants and producers.

Gary Jones, Executive Head Chef, Le Manoir aux Quat'Saisons

010
ARROW MILL HOTEL

Arrow, Near Alcester, Warwickshire, B49 5NL

01789 762419
www.arrowmill.com

A rrow Mill doesn't care for food miles. From the windows of the spectacular and secluded riverside restaurant, diners can observe chef Simon Woodhams' larder.

In the surrounding fields, Dexter cattle live a natural life grazing on fresh pasture. Bresse, Welsummer and Barnevelder chickens provide a daily supply of golden yolked eggs. The local farmer grows fields full of England's finest asparagus, a vegetable garden provides fresh herbs and greenery, while the nearby Black Pig Company rears delicious, succulent Berkshire black pigs.

Self-taught Simon moved to Arrow Mill with his wife, Agnes, 28 years ago. They created a temple to fresh, seasonal ingredients. Dishes burst with flavour and are immaculately presented. Menus are rooted in the classics. Garden spinach is paired with crispy hens eggs, house-smoked pigeon breast is presented with salt-baked beetroot, walnuts and air-dried ham and local pork racks sit beside hickory-smoked cheeks and a sticky gravy.

"We have some of the best producers in the country, right on our doorstep," says Simon. "The restaurant showcases the finest flavours."

Arrow Mill is a remarkable venue in which to dine. It was a working flour mill for more than a thousand years and was valued as three shillings and six pence when it was mentioned in the Domesday Book. Flour was ground until the early 1950s and it was not until 1966 that the venue opened as a restaurant. The Mill's wheel has been completely refurbished and provides a fresh water feed to the lake.

Arrow Mill is a family affair and Simon's son, James, helps to run the kitchen. He stays true to the family tradition – it's a recipe that has served the Woodhams, and Arrow Mill, with distinction.

Diners at Arrow Mill enjoy thrilling views across Warwickshire countryside, with tables positioned in a light and airy room. Father and son Simon and James Woodhams take care to provide food that befits such an elegant setting. Simon says: "The views are spectacular and we want our food to be just as special. Our ingredients are often harvested from the land that diners can see from their windows. Local food doesn't get any better than here at Arrow Mill."

NEW INN LANE ASPARAGUS, CRISPY HEN'S EGG, BLACK PIG CURED HAM & HOLLANDAISE

SERVES 4

🍷 *Sauvignon Blanc, Babich Black Label, 2010 (New Zealand)*

Method

For The Perfectly Poached Crispy Hen's Egg

Place a large saucepan onto the heat and three-quarters fill with water. Bring to a gentle boil and add the white wine vinegar. Forget about stirring the boiling water around.

For perfect poached eggs every time get the freshest eggs you can. Crack the hen's eggs one at a time into the water and cook for around four to five minutes. Make sure the yolks are still soft, then refresh in cold water. Drain on kitchen towel and coat in breadcrumbs.

Deep fry the eggs at 180°C until they're golden brown.

For The Asparagus

Snap off the base of each stem and trim so that all the stems are the same size. Using a peeler, peel from the base all the way down and round. Drop the asparagus into a separate pan of boiling salted water for a couple of minutes until tender.

For The Hollandaise Sauce

Place the egg yolks into a metal bowl along with the vinegar and place over a pan of simmering water. Whisk the eggs until they have formed a *sabayon*. Then, slowly add the butter, whisking all the time. Remove from the heat and check the seasoning. Reserve somewhere warm until required.

For The Dried Ham Crisp

Lay half the dried ham onto a sheet of parchment paper on a baking tray. Place in oven for 30 minutes on medium and then let cool. Keep half the cured ham for plating.

Chef's Tip

This dish showcases seasonal flavours at their absolute best. So go the extra mile when you're sourcing your ingredients and make sure everything is as fresh and local as possible. You'll be rewarded by delicious, seasonal flavours.

To Serve

Serve as pictured.

Ingredients

Asparagus

1 proper round of asparagus

Hollandaise Sauce

2 free range egg yolks
25ml white wine vinegar
200g butter (melted)
seasoning

'Ham And Eggs'

100ml white wine vinegar
4 free range 'laid that day' hen's eggs
Panko breadcrumbs
8 slices Parma style cured ham

CRUMB TOPPED DAY BOAT COD LOIN, TAGLIOLINI VEGETABLES & GRAIN MUSTARD BUTTER SAUCE

SERVES 4

 *Chateaux les Tuileries - Entre-deux-Mers 2011
(France)*

Ingredients

Cod Loin And Crumb Topping

4 x 140g cod fillets
vegetable oil
1 lemon (squeeze of)
salt and pepper
white breadcrumbs
50g butter
grated parmesan cheese
1 shallot
1 sprig flat leaf parsley

small carton or can of chopped tomato sauce

Grain Mustard Butter Sauce

1 shallot
1 garlic clove
1 sprig thyme
100ml white wine vinegar
100ml white wine
100ml double cream
250g butter
1 tbsp farmhouse grain mustard

Vegetable Tagliolini

1 box of the best tagliolini pasta you can buy
1 carrot
1 stick celery
1 courgette
1 leek (pulled out of the garden)
knob of butter
lemon juice (squeeze of)
1 handful chives (chopped)

Garnish

handful small spinach leaves
1 tbsp popped broad beans or edamame beans
a generous handful of garden peas

Method

For The Cod Loin Fillets

Wash and dry the cod and make sure there are no pin bones left in the fillet.

For The Grain Mustard Butter Sauce

Peel the shallot and garlic and dice finely. Place into a saucepan along with the thyme, vinegar and wine.

Place onto the heat and reduce by half, then add the cream and bring up to a boil. Turn down the heat and slowly add the butter, stirring all the time.

Once all the butter is combined, finish with the chives and grain mustard and season. Place aside until needed.

For The Crumb Topping

Briefly blitz the breadcrumbs, butter, cheese, shallot and parsley in a processor until it comes together. Season with salt and pepper and a squeeze of lemon juice.

> **Chef's Tip**
>
> I always use fresh breadcrumbs. That gives it the best texture.

For The Vegetable Tagliolini

Julienne the carrot, celery, courgette and leek finely. B*lanch* all the vegetables in a saucepan of boiling salted water. Add the pasta either before or after, dependent on cooking time.

Drain off the water, add a good knob of butter and a squeeze of lemon juice.

Check the seasoning and finish with a handful of chopped chives.

To Finish The Cod

Preheat the oven to 165°C. Place the cod loins on a lightly oiled oven tray and top with the tomato sauce, followed by the crumb mix topping. Place into the oven for six minutes.

Once cooked, remove the cod from the oven and place one fillet onto each pile of the pasta and vegetables. Spoon the sauce around the cod.

DATE PUDDING, WALNUT BRITTLE & SALT CARAMEL SAUCE

SERVES 6

 Willowglen Gewürztraminer 2011
(Australia)

Ingredients

Date Pudding

200g dried dates (stoned and chopped)
250ml black tea (not too strong)
1/2 tsp bicarbonate soda
85g unsalted butter (softened)
175g self raising flour
1 tsp mixed spice
175g golden caster sugar
2 eggs
6 (10cm x 6cm) ramekins or dariole moulds

Walnut Brittle

50g walnuts
125g caster sugar

Caramel Sauce

50g butter
sea salt
250g caster sugar
142ml double cream
4 tbsp water

To Serve

cream, crème fraîche or ice cream

Method

For The Pudding

Preheat the oven to 180°C. Butter and flour six ramekins or *dariole* moulds.

Mix the butter and sugar together, then slowly add two beaten eggs. Fold in the sieved flour and set aside.

Meanwhile, mix the bicarbonate of soda and tea and pour this over the dates. Mix well, allow to cool for ten minutes and then pour into the creamed pudding mixture. Bring together to create a runny batter. Pour into the prepared moulds and bake for 40 minutes or until springy to touch.

For The Walnut Brittle

Scatter the nuts onto a baking sheet and place into a preheated oven at 180°C. Leave for six to ten minutes, until golden but not burned. Let them cool a little then, while still warm, rub off the skins.

Tip the sugar into a heavy bottomed, wide pan. Add a splash of water and gently warm over a low heat until the sugar has dissolved. Do not stir. Continue heating until the sugar achieves a light brown colour. Do not burn. Add the nuts.

Quickly pour the mixture onto a heat proof mat and allow to cool until it is semi-hard. Then, use a circular cutter – the size will depend on the thickness of your brittle – and cut through. Allow to cool completely, then lift discs of brittle from heat proof mat.

For The Caramel Sauce

Tip the sugar into a heavy bottomed frying pan, stir in four tablespoons of water, then place over a medium heat until the sugar has dissolved. Turn up the heat and bubble for four to five minutes until you have caramel. Remove from heat, then carefully stir in the cream and butter. Leave the sauce to cool.

To Serve

Plate as pictured and serve with cream, crème fraîche or ice cream.

> **Chef's Tip**
>
> If you're looking for a shortcut, you can use the tried and tested 'all-ingredients-in-one-bowl' food processor method when you're making the pudding. Just don't tell your guests!

020
BIBURY COURT

Bibury, Cirencester, Gloucestershire, GL7 5NT

01285 740 337
www.biburycourt.com

Bibury Court hotel is a beautiful Jacobean Cotswold mansion that dates back to the early part of the 17th Century. It sits in acres of garden and parkland with paths that link into the village itself, surely one of the most photographed in the whole of the UK. Bibury village was named in 2013 as one of the 'Top ten coolest small towns in Europe*'. Dining at Bibury Court is as fine as the house, serving modern British food without pretension.

The Oak Room is an intimate and sophisticated restaurant presided over by chef Adam Montgomery. A rising star on the culinary scene, Adam has been awarded two AA Rosettes for his modern British cuisine. The à la carte menu changes with the seasons to reflect the best of the high quality produce available in the Cotswolds and surrounding areas. Adam and his team are meticulous when it comes to marrying flavour, texture and taste on the plate, much to the delight of his growing legion of fans.

With 18 bedrooms, a roaring fire in the drawing room on cold days, snug bar, award-winning restaurant and glorious gardens bordered by the trout-filled river Coln, the hotel ticks every box for a night or two away. It is a perfect base from which to explore the beauty of the Cotswolds or to enjoy a romantic break. It's also a popular stop for lunch and afternoon tea. On a Summer's day, sitting in Bibury Court's extensive gardens, afternoon tea is as quintessentially and delightfully British as you can get. Or how about a bread-making course, presided over by the owners of the famed organic 'Shipton Mill' who also own Bibury Court, and supply their acclaimed artisan breads UK-wide.

*Fox News US

Relish the region's exclusive offers.
See page 003 for details.

Head chef Adam Montgomery's style is sophisticated, but earthy, modern British food without pretension. The depth of ingredients and flavour is carried to the plates, with stunning interpretations of classic dishes. Always adapting to the seasons and to nature itself, his food has evolved to a modern British base. His menus reflect those beliefs and the food is served without pretension, fuss and with the produce taking centre stage. Chef Adam lets the quality of produce and the talent in his brigade speak for itself.

LEAF SMOKED PIGEON, LIVER PARFAIT, HAZELNUTS, PORT, FRANGELICO, BRIOCHE

SERVES 4

 Gruner Veltliner 2010 Spiegel, Weingut Hiedler Kemptal (Austria)

Ingredients

Smoked Pigeon

4 pigeon breasts
handful dry Autumn leaves
handful wood chips

Liver Parfait

10 pigeon livers
500g chicken livers
75ml port
3 egg yolks
250g butter
1 clove garlic
salt
10ml hazelnut oil
5ml vegetable oil

Frangelico Jelly

250ml stock syrup (150g sugar, 350g water
reduced to 250ml)
100ml Frangelico
4 gelatine leaves
3.5g agar agar

Brioche

450g strong flour
20g yeast
70ml water
4 eggs
salt (pinch of)
50g caster sugar
100g soft butter

Garnish

100g hazelnuts (crushed)
micro cress
red wine *reduction* (optional)

Method

For The Parfait

Heat the vegetable oil in a medium sized heavy bottomed pan, add the garlic and gently colour before adding the chicken and pigeon livers. Cook for two to three minutes. Add port and reduce for 20 seconds then remove from heat. When cool, place in a food processor and blend, then add the eggs. Once incorporated, slowly add the melted butter and hazelnut oil. Blend until combined and then pass through a sieve into a container. Place in a fridge to set.

For The Brioche

Place the flour, yeast, sugar, salt, water and eggs into the bowl of an electric mixer and mix until a smooth dough has been formed. Slowly add the soft butter to the dough, making sure that the butter is completely incorporated. Once all the butter has been added to the mix, remove from the bowl and portion into 150g pieces. Place into 30g mini loaf tins and leave somewhere warm to prove until the dough reaches the top of the tin. Cook at 160°C for approximately 25 minutes.

For The Frangelico Jelly

Heat the stock syrup and Frangelico. Place the gelatine in a bowl of cold water to bloom. When the liquid is at a gentle boil, add the agar agar. Cook for one minute then remove from the heat. Set on a large, flat plate and place in the fridge to set until needed.

For The Smoked Pigeon

Place the leaves and wood chips in a roasting tray and put into the oven at 180°C for 15 minutes. Place an old coffee cup upside down in the tray with a cooling wire rested on top. Lay the pigeon breasts on the cooling wire and cover the tray with tinfoil. Return to oven for six minutes. Remove the pigeon from the cooling wire and let them rest for five minutes.

To Serve

Arrange as in picture and garnish with micro cress and hazelnuts.

ROAST HARE NOSE TO TAIL

SERVES 4

 Barbera d'Alba 2009 Pio Cesare
(Piedmont, Italy)

Ingredients

Roast Hare

1 whole hare
1 garlic bulb
sprig thyme
vegetable oil (enough to cover)

Red Wine Sauce

200ml beef stock
100ml chicken stock
50ml red wine
1 shallot
2 cloves garlic
1 celery stick

Tortellini Pasta

115g '00' flour
1 whole egg
2 egg yolks

Butternut Squash Purée

250g butternut squash
75g butter
200ml water
salt
sprig thyme
2g xantham gum

Almond Purée

75g flaked almonds
150ml whole milk
1g xantham gum

Chestnut Paste

100g chestnuts (*blanched*)
50ml Crème de Cacao

Garnish

2 baby turnip
4 baby carrots
4 baby leeks
4 baby beetroot
50g Panko breadcrumbs
50g honey mustard

Method

For The Hare

Break the hare down into joints - hind legs, front legs, loins and racks. Bone and roll the hind legs, cook at 90°C for six hours, then chill. In a pan, add the front legs, one bulb of garlic (split) and a good sprig of thyme. Cover in vegetable oil and *confit* slowly for four to five hours until tender. Remove from oil and shred. Season and allow to cool. Trim the loins of all sinew and fat and set aside. *French trim* the first two cutlets from each rack (the fat end) and set aside.

For The Red Wine Sauce

Fry the vegetables until coloured. Add the beef and chicken stock with the red wine and reduce.

For The Pasta

Sift the flour into a bowl with a pinch of salt. Add the eggs and combine to a smooth dough. Wrap and chill for 20 minutes. Roll through a pasta machine to thickness setting two and place onto a lightly floured surface. Cut out discs 120mm in diameter. Take a tablespoon of *confit* leg and place in the centre of the pasta disc and form discs into tortellini and refrigerate.

For The Chestnut Paste

Add all the ingredients to a blender and mix until smooth. Refrigerate.

For The Butternut Purée

Peel and dice the squash into 4 x 2.5cm cubes. Add to a pan with the butter, water, salt and thyme and cook until tender. Blend, slowly adding the xantham gum to create a perfectly smooth purée. Season.

For The Almond Purée

Bring the milk and almonds to a boil, then simmer for five minutes until soft. Blend, then slowly add the xantham gum. Season.

For The Garnish

Place turnip into a pan of cold water and cook until tender. Repeat with carrots and beetroot, refresh and set aside. *Blanch* the leeks in boiling water for one minute. Clean and trim all vegetables whilst chilling for a perfect finish.

To Serve

Now to bring it all together - on a tray, season the hare components with salt. Heat a little oil in a pan and sear the loin for approximately one to two minutes each side. Then, add the cutlets and slices of hind leg and colour. Remove and allow to rest. In a pan of boiling water, *blanch* the tortellini for three to four minutes. *Blanch* the baby vegetables in salted water for one minute, drain and season. Warm the purées and get creative!

CHOCOLATE & HAZELNUT MOUSSE, CROUSTILLANT, BABY PEAR, MILK ICE CREAM, CANDY FLOSS

SERVES 4

 Banyuls Rouge Les Dorde Pauilles, Château de Jau (France)

Ingredients

Croustillant

125g pancakes (dried)
275g flaked almonds (roasted)
250g butter
85g cocoa nibs

Praline Mousse

30ml hazelnut oil
300g praline paste
150g milk chocolate
50g dark chocolate
140g egg yolk
140g sugar
75ml water
1ltr double cream
1 vanilla pod

Milk Ice Cream

200ml stock syrup (100g sugar, 100ml water)
2 tins condensed milk
675ml milk

Baby Pear

4 baby pears
200g honey
200g light brown sugar
75g butter

Candy Floss

make as instructed by machine manufacturer

Method

For The Milk Ice Cream

Place stock syrup, milk and condensed milk into a pan and bring to a boil. Put the ice cream in an ice cream machine or a tub in the freezer and stir every 20 minutes until set.

For The Croustillant

Preheat oven to 200°C. Finely chop all dry ingredients into a bowl and bind with the melted butter. Add the cocoa nibs to the mixture and spread evenly on a tray to approximately 1cm in thickness. Cook in the oven for approximately ten minutes.

For The Praline Mousse

Melt the chocolate and praline paste together, then add the hazelnut oil. Put the sugar and water into a pan and heat to 121°C. Whisk the egg yolks to ribbon stage, then slowly pour in the hot sugar whilst continuing to whisk. Split the vanilla pod and add to the cream and whip to soft peak. Mix the egg yolk and sugar mix with the cream and add the chocolate mix. Place into the fridge to set for two hours.

For The Baby Pear

Put the sugar, honey and butter in the pan and boil until a golden caramel is achieved. Add the pears to the caramel and continue to boil for five minutes, stirring continuously. Remove from the heat and set aside to cool down before removing pears from the caramel.

For The Candy Floss

Follow the manufacturers instructions to make the candy floss.

To Serve

Arrange as pictured.

030
BUCKLAND MANOR

Buckland, Gloucestershire, WR12 7LY

01386 852 626
www.bucklandmanor.co.uk

B uckland Manor, privately owned by Andrew and Christina Brownsword, is a special hotel tucked inconspicuously in a tranquil corner of the village of Buckland, nestled next to the ancient village church. Once you discover it, you will not want to leave.

In the heart of the Cotswold tourist trail, Buckland is only a few minutes from the much loved town of Broadway, with its pretty high street and eclectic shops. Those who stay in Buckland are well placed to discover the wider area of the Cotswolds, Oxford's dreaming spires and the home of Shakespeare, Stratford-upon-Avon. Visitors can explore during the day and return to relax in the luxurious surroundings.

Whether visitors are looking for a romantic getaway, somewhere for a special event or celebration, or a quiet escape, this quintessentially English luxury hotel will not disappoint.

Befitting a luxury hotel, every detail is considered at Buckland Manor. Friendly and welcoming faces greet visitors, the smell of freshly cut flowers permeates the air, genuine warmth and a wonderful atmosphere fills the elegant rooms - the scene is set for total relaxation.

Views from the windows over the gardens delight and in the Summer the vibrant greens of the lawns and trees blend seamlessly with the rolling hills beyond.

The elegant public rooms are ideal places to sit back, relax and simply enjoy some 'down time' - read a book, indulge in an afternoon tea or play a game of Scrabble.

The overall experience at Buckland Manor will be reminiscent of visiting the rather wonderful home of a very good friend, one who has the art of warm hospitality perfectly honed to ensure that your visit is enjoyable in every way.

Relish the region's exclusive offers.
See page 003 for details.

At Buckland Manor, the superb cuisine has won many accolades over the years, the restaurant continues to attract connoisseurs of fine food and wine from around the world. Menus feature fresh local produce from the neighbouring Vale of Evesham, affectionately known as the market garden of England. Fresh herbs are grown in the Manor's own grounds and, as you would expect in a house of this heritage, there is a magnificent wine cellar.

SALT BAKED CELERIAC MOUSSE, HERITAGE BEETROOT, TRUFFLE DRESSING, WALNUT PUREE

SERVES 4

 Chenin Blanc 2008 Pithon-Paille Coteau des Treilles (France)

Ingredients

Salt Baked Celeriac Mousse

20g sea salt
20g table salt
400g plain flour
285ml water
300g celeriac
200ml double cream
2 x 5g agar agar
3 gelatine leaves (bronze leaf)
small sprig thyme

Truffle Dressing

175ml truffle juice
80ml groundnut oil
3ml Xeres vinegar
5g salt
13ml lemon juice
2g ground white pepper

Walnut Purée

100g walnuts
200ml apple juice

Heritage Beetroot

100g cooked beetroot (sliced)
2 ltr water
300ml white wine vinegar
250ml honey
5g Chinese five spice
100ml olive oil
50g shallots (sliced)
bay leaf
10 white peppercorns
45g salt

Garnish

micro herbs
sliced fresh truffle (optional)

Method

For The Salt Baked Celeriac Mousse (Prepare the day before)

Place salt and flour in a mixing bowl. Add water to bring it together as a dough.

Wrap the dough around the celeriac making sure it's sealed. Bake for 50 minutes at 160°C and rest for the same time.

Soak the gelatine in a small bowl of cold water.

Remove the dough casing. Purée the celeriac and add the double cream and add the agar agar. On a medium heat, bring the purée to 65°C.

Squeeze the water from the gelatine leaves and add them to the purée with the thyme. Pass the purée through a sieve into moulds. Set them in the fridge for approximately four hours.

> **Chef's Tip**
>
> The mousse is best made a day in advance of serving, to help it set and make it easier to cut.

For The Walnut Purée

Place walnuts and apple juice in a pan and bring to a boil over a medium heat. Purée the mixture until smooth.

For The Truffle Dressing

Mix all of the ingredients together in a bowl and pour into a bottle.

For The Heritage Beetroot

Sweat the shallots on a low heat but be careful not to let them colour. Add the remaining ingredients, excluding the beetroot and bring to a boil. Cook for ten minutes. Reduce the liquid by half, then pour on top of the beetroot to marinade for two hours.

To Serve

Place mousse onto the middle of the plate. Swipe the walnut purée to the right of the mousse. Build the beetroot salad around. Dress with the truffle dressing and micro herbs. Some sliced fresh truffle would also be a luxurious optional extra. You can also decorate your plate with a simple beetroot purée, or make vegetable crisps, which add height to the dish.

LOIN OF TODDINGTON LAMB, SPRING WILD GARLIC, CHANTERELLE MUSHROOMS, SHEPHERD'S PIE, ROSEMARY JUS

SERVES 4

🍷 *Villa Mottura 2010, Primitivo di Manduria (Italy)*

Ingredients

The Lamb

300g lamb loin
330g lamb shoulder
150g belly of lamb
sea salt
2 ltr *confit* oil
3 shallots
2 tbsp mint sauce
4 cloves garlic
150g unsalted butter
handful chives (chopped)
1 tbsp ras el hanout
100ml veal glace
vegetable oil
1 large Maris Piper potato

Spring Wild Garlic

200g wild garlic leaf (finely chopped)
150ml water
1 shallot
1 clove garlic
50g butter
1 spring onion

Rosemary Jus

150g fresh rosemary
1 ltr chicken stock
500ml veal glace
3 shallots
2 cloves garlic
375ml red wine
3 tomatoes
1 tsp cumin powder
1 tbsp tomato purée
2 celery stalks

Vegetables

50g fresh Chanterelle mushrooms
100g purple sprouting broccoli

Method

For The Rosemary Jus

Sweat off the vegetables in a heavy-bottomed pan until soft and a little coloured. Add the rosemary and cumin powder. Add red wine and reduce by half. Add the chicken stock. Simmer and reduce this by half again. In a separate pan, reduce the veal glace down by two thirds until thick. When done, combine the two liquids and pass through a fine sieve. Set aside and keep warm.

For The Lamb (Prepare the day before)

Season the lamb shoulder and belly with sea salt for 24 hours. Wash the salt off and place in an ovenproof pan and cover with the *confit* oil. Place a sheet of foil over the top and cook at 130°C for six hours until tender.

Trim any sinew off the lamb loin. Mince the trimmings, shoulder and belly. Place the mince in a heavy-bottomed pan and sweat the mince meat. Dice and add the shallots and garlic. Stir in 10g of butter, be careful not to brown the shallots and garlic. Add the mint sauce, ras el hanout and chopped chives. Season with salt and pepper. Add 100ml veal glace. Place the mixture in a small sided tray and press. Refrigerate for six hours until set.

For The Shepherd's Pie

Once set, cut into strips approximately 8cm by 1.5cm. Peel the Maris Piper and cut into matchstick size pieces (we use a Japanese turning slicer to achieve this). Salt and squeeze the potato in a cloth to extract excess water. Wrap around the lamb mix and cook in a deep fat fryer at 160°C until golden brown.

To Finish The Lamb Loin

Season lamb loin and place in a light frying pan with a small amount of vegetable oil and colour on both sides for approximately two minutes each side. Place in an oven at 160°C for two minutes. Rest for two minutes before slicing.

For The Spring Wild Garlic

Slice one shallot, the spring onion and one clove of garlic and sweat in a pan, be careful not to colour. Add 150ml water and simmer. Add finely chopped garlic leaves and purée the mixture. Add 50g of butter until smooth then pass through a fine sieve. Keep warm until you are ready to serve.

For The Vegetables

Blanch purple sprouting broccoli and mushrooms in a seasoned pan of water.

To Serve

Swipe the garlic purée on the plate and place the cooked lamb on top of this. Cut the bottom of your cooked shepherd's pie off and stand it next to the lamb. Place the purple sprouting and mushrooms around the plate. Pour the rosemary *jus* over and around or serve on the side if desired.

VANILLA & RHUBARB CHEESECAKE, MILLE-FEUILLE, RHUBARB JELLY & SORBET

SERVES 4

 Chateau Suduiraut 1996 Sauternes (France)

Ingredients

Cheesecake

250g digestive biscuits
50g butter
125g white chocolate
1 vanilla pod
650g cream cheese
280g mascarpone
190g caster sugar
500ml double cream

Jelly

50g rhubarb
icing sugar (to taste)
10g caster sugar
5 gelatine leaves, or 6g (soaked in water for approximately 20 mins)
1g agar agar
lemon juice (squeeze of)

4 x 7^1/$_2$cm *dariole* moulds

Sorbet

200g rhubarb
200g caster sugar
200ml water
1 vanilla pod
lemon juice (squeeze of)

Mille-Feuille

2 sheets of brick pastry
1 egg
icing sugar (to taste)
100g rhubarb (cut into batons)
100g caster sugar
350ml water
^{1}/$_2$ vanilla pod
lemon juice (squeeze of)
100ml sweetened double cream (whipped)

Chef's Tip

To ensure a light, smooth texture don't whip the cream into cheesecake mixture.

Method

For The Cheesecake Base

Melt the butter and the white chocolate together over a gentle heat. Crush the digestive biscuits and add the melted butter and chocolate to the biscuits. Place mixture into the bottom of a lined mould and press it down.

For The Cheesecake Filling

Split the vanilla pod in half and scrape the vanilla seeds from the middle. Place the mascarpone, cream cheese, 190g of caster sugar and vanilla seeds into a mixing bowl and beat together.

Whip and gently fold in 450ml of the double cream. Squeeze excess water from the gelatine and warm 50ml of the remaining cream before adding and folding. Take the mould with the biscuit base and place the mixture on top of the biscuits. Set in fridge for at least two hours.

For The Rhubarb Jelly

Place 50g rhubarb, the lemon juice, icing sugar, 10g caster sugar and 25ml water in a metal bowl. Clingfilm the bowl very tightly. Place the bowl over a *bain-marie* for two hours. Make sure the water in the pan is topped up, but not touching the bottom of your metal bowl.

Leave the bowl to cool completely.

Remove the clingfilm and pass the rhubarb through a *chinois*. Add the 6g or five sheets of gelatine to 300ml of the liquid with 1g of agar agar. Let it cool but while it is still pourable, pour a thin layer on top of the cheesecake and set in the fridge for two hours.

For The Rhubarb Sorbet

Place all the ingredients into a pan. Cook on a low heat for approximately 20 minutes. Remove the vanilla pod. Blend the liquid and pass through *chinois* and let the mixture cool and churn in an ice cream machine.

For The Mille-Feuille

Take two sheets of the brick pastry and brush a light egg wash between the two sheets. Cut into 1.5cm by 8cm stripes. Place on to a tray lined with baking parchment and dust with icing sugar. Bake for four minutes at 175°C until golden brown.

Poach batons of rhubarb in a mixture of 100g sugar and 350ml water and half a vanilla pod squeeze of lemon juice until just soft.

To Serve

Take the cheesecake from the mould and cut to required size and shape. Whisk up a small amount of sweetened double cream and place into a piping bag. Place cheesecake on the plate. Next to it place a tower made up of the poached rhubarb, sweetened cream and brick pastry. Dust with a little icing sugar to finish.
Serve with the homemade rhubarb sorbet.

040
THE DINING ROOM & COTSWOLD GRILL

Cotswold House Hotel and Spa, The Square, Chipping Campden, Gloucestershire, GL55 6AN

01386 840 330
www.cotswoldhouse.com

Cotswold House hotel restaurant and luxury spa, in the heart of picturesque Chipping Campden, is a luxury townhouse, boutique style hotel, the cosy Dining Room Restaurant and Cotswold Grill. Tranquillity, comfort, exceptional food and the stunning Cotswold Spa await you.

Secluded gardens and their cottage suites, some with private jacuzzi spa, make the Cotswold House a favoured retreat for culinary couples seeking a country break in the heart of the region. The hotel is a member of Mr & Mrs Smith and features in both Sawdays Special Places and Gourmet-Lifestyle guides.

It has two dining experiences - the elegant Dining Room and more informal Cotswold Grill - both of which showcase the skills of the chef brigade.

The contemporary style makes the Cotswold House Hotel one of the most admired boutique hotels in the Cotswolds, promising a warm welcome and exceptional personal service.

The menu is designed around a variety of dishes, featuring different flavours and cooking techniques, largely sourced from the region, with simple combinations that complement and enhance each other. The style is balanced, light and seasonal (of course!) and the food served is rustic, but neat. Service is without pretension, simple with the emphasis on attention to detail and the atmosphere is relaxed, even when it's a special occasion.

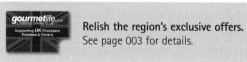

Relish the region's exclusive offers.
See page 003 for details.

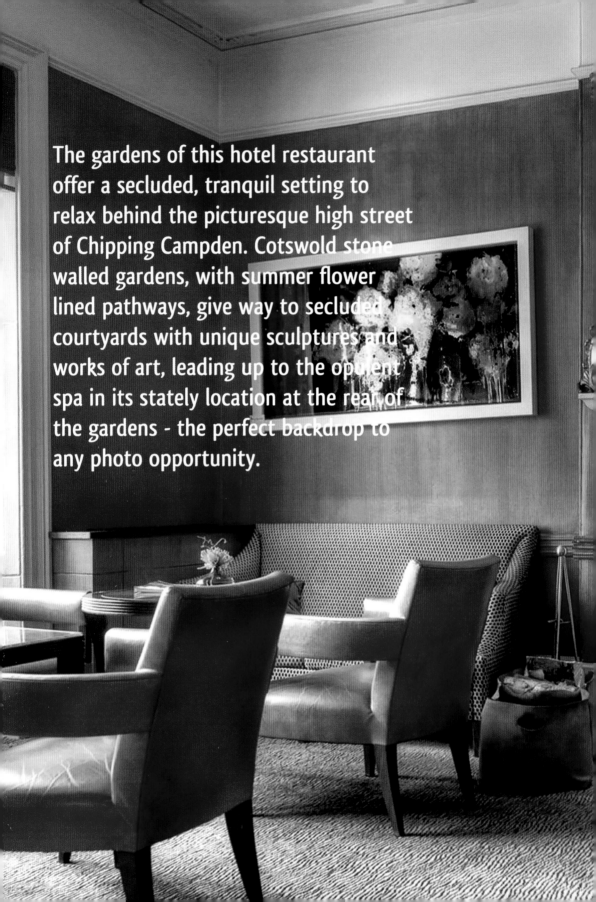

The gardens of this hotel restaurant offer a secluded, tranquil setting to relax behind the picturesque high street of Chipping Campden. Cotswold stone walled gardens, with summer flower lined pathways, give way to secluded courtyards with unique sculptures and works of art, leading up to the opulent spa in its stately location at the rear of the gardens - the perfect backdrop to any photo opportunity.

PICKLED BABY BEETROOT, GOAT'S CHEESE MOUSSE & FRESH BLOOD ORANGE

SERVES 4

🍷 *TYDY Sauvignon Blanc 2011
(Loire, France)*

Ingredients

Pickled Beetroot

2 bunches baby beetroot
100ml water
100ml white wine vinegar
50g sugar

Goat's Cheese Mousse

250g goat's cheese
100g double cream
salt and pepper

Blood Orange Gel

200ml blood orange juice
25g vegetable gel

Garnish

1 bunch watercress
1 blood orange

Method

For The Pickled Beetroot (Make at least 24 hours before)

Wash beetroot under cold water to remove any soil, then place into a pan of cold water and bring to a simmer. Cook until tender, which should take about 30 to 45 minutes, depending on size of the beetroot.

Once cooked, leave in the cooking water to slightly cool until you can handle the beetroot and rub off the skin.

Add the sugar, water and vinegar into a large pan and bring to a boil, making sure the sugar has dissolved. Add the peeled beetroot to the hot pickling liquor and allow to cool. Store in an airtight container until ready for use.

For best results keep in the pickling liquor for 24 hours.

> **Chef's Tip**
>
> The best types of beetroot to use are reds, golden or candy. When purchasing, look for beetroot that is about the size of a ping-pong ball.

For The Goat's Cheese Mousse

Cut the rind off the goat's cheese and blend in a food processor until smooth. Add the cream and blend until the cream has slightly whipped - this will not take long (be careful not to over whip). Add salt and pepper to your taste.

Place into a container and set in to fridge for two to three hours.

For The Blood Orange Gel

Whisk together the blood orange juice and vegetable gel until the powder has been incorporated. Bring to a boil and set in a container and leave to cool. Once cool, blend in a liquidiser until smooth and place into a container for later.

To Serve

Segment the orange - take a sharp knife and cut the top and bottom off the orange. Then remove the rest of the orange zest and cut in between the segments until they come loose. Remove any pips. Pick the watercress into nice little bunches. Scoop a ball of the goat's cheese mousse with a warm ice cream scoop or spoon and arrange all the elements of the dish as pictured.

CHARGRILLED FILLET OF BEEF, POTATO FONDANT, BRAISED RED CABBAGE, WILD MUSHROOMS

SERVES 4

 Barbera d'alba 2009 Piedmont Bava
(Italy)

Ingredients

4 x 6oz fillets beef
salt and pepper

Red Cabbage

500g red cabbage (thinly sliced)
150ml malt vinegar
200ml red wine
125g sugar
$1/4$ stick fresh cinnamon

Mushroom Purée

1kg button mushrooms
100ml vegetable oil
1 clove garlic
2 banana shallots
100ml vegetable stock
50ml Madeira
150ml double cream
salt and pepper

Potato Fondant

150g unsalted butter
4 large maris piper potatoes
500ml chicken stock

Wild Mushrooms

250g wild mushrooms
15ml olive oil, knob of butter
salt and pepper, lemon juice (squeeze of)

Garnish

watercress

Chef's Tip

When the mushrooms are cooked, add a small amount of lemon juice - this will add the acidity needed to the final dish.

Method

For The Red Cabbage

Bring the wine, vinegar, sugar and cinnamon stick to a boil. Add the thinly sliced cabbage to the boiled liquid and cook slowly until the cabbage is tender.

For The Mushroom Purée

Rub the vegetable oil over the button mushrooms and roast in a hot oven (180°C) until golden brown. Peel and slice the shallots and garlic and place into a hot pan with a little oil and slightly colour. *Deglaze* with the Madeira and reduce until most of the liquid has gone.

Separately, bring the vegetable stock to a boil and add to the shallots. Fry the mushrooms until golden, drain and add to the stock. Bring back to a boil and add the double cream. Boil once again then blend until smooth. Add salt and pepper to your taste. For a smoother finish, pass the purée though a fine sieve.

For The Potato Fondant

Peel and cut the potatoes to the shape you would like your fondants to be (it does the help in the cooking process if they are all the same size).

Slice the butter and place into a cold pan. Add the potatoes then place onto a moderate heat. Cook until the bottom of the potatoes are golden brown - be careful not to burn the butter. Add a small amount of chicken stock - be careful as this will bubble a lot. Keep on the heat until the stock has reduced and the butter is foaming. Turn the potatoes over and repeat this process. The fondants are cooked when a knife can be easily inserted into the potato. If the potatoes are not cooked, add more stock and reduce again. This process can be repeated until cooked.

For The Wild Mushrooms

To prepare the mushrooms, cut into small pieces and wash in cold water to remove any soil. Drain and dry with paper towel. Preheat a frying pan, add a small amount of oil and fry the mushrooms half way though. Add a knob of butter and season with salt and pepper.

For The Fillet Of Beef

Preheat the oven to 180°C. Season the beef with salt and pepper and preheat a large frying pan. Colour the fillet until golden brown all over then place onto a tray in the oven. This should take six to eight minutes for medium rare.

To Serve

Plate as pictured.

VANILLA PANNA COTTA, RUM ROASTED PINEAPPLE, CARAMELISED WHITE CHOCOLATE

SERVES 4

 *Banyuls Rouge Chateau de Jau 2008
(France)*

Ingredients

Panna Cotta

1 vanilla pod
225ml double cream
75ml semi-skimmed milk
180g caster sugar
1 gelatine leaf
(supermarkets normally sell them in
half leaves so use 2 in this case)

Roasted Pineapple

1 pineapple
140g brown sugar
pinch salt and pepper
3 limes (zest and juice)
70ml dark rum

Caramelised White Chocolate

200g white chocolate (good quality)

Method

For The Panna Cotta

Take the vanilla pod and spilt down the middle to scrape out the seeds. Add the pods, seeds, milk, cream and sugar into a large heavy bottomed pan and heat until hot. Remove from the heat (do not boil).

Soak the gelatine in cold water until soft. Add the gelatine to the cream mix and stir well until the gelatine is all incorporated.

Remove the vanilla pod.

Pour the mix into a bowl and place on top of another bowl of iced water.

Keep stirring the mix every couple of minutes until it thickens. Stirring will keep the vanilla seeds spread evenly throughout the mix and prevent them from sinking to the bottom of the moulds.

Pour the mix into 100ml moulds and store in the fridge until set.

For The Roasted Pineapple

Top and tail the pineapple with a sharp knife. Cut the side of the pineapple off, removing all of the skin. Cut into quarters and remove the core with a knife.

Add all other ingredients into a pan and bring to a boil. Once boiled, pour over the pineapple ensuring the liquid covers the pineapple and leave for an hour to marinade.

Remove the pineapple from the liquid and roast in the oven at 220°C for 15 minutes.

For The Caramelised White Chocolate

Preheat oven to 140°C.

Place the chocolate onto a small metal tray or into a small casserole bowl. Place over a pan of boiling water and stir the chocolate every five minutes until the chocolate has caramelised. This should be a light golden brown colour.

Now pour the melted mixture onto greaseproof paper and spread thinly then leave to cool.

Once set, break into small pieces for decoration.

To Serve

Plate as pictured.

050
ECKINGTON MANOR

Hammock Road, Eckington, Worcestershire, WR10 3BJ

01386 751 600
www.eckingtonmanor.co.uk

The Restaurant at Eckington Manor opened in Spring 2013 as a natural extension to the hugely successful Eckington Manor luxury accommodation and cookery school. Situated in the Vale of Evesham, the chefs, under the expert guidance of Judy Gardner, have access to some of the UK's best seasonal produce and really are spoilt for choice during the local asparagus festival. As well as this abundance of local fayre, Judy farms her own Aberdeen Angus and Highland beef on the estate's 260 acres of land. Food provenance and traceability is at the heart of her ethos and, in her relatively short career as a farmer, she has made quite an impact. Her beef is of superior quality and is hung for 30 days to give it a distinctive flavour and marbling.

Eckington Manor is the perfect retreat from which to explore the Cotswolds. The 15 bedrooms have been awarded five star gold accreditation by Visit Britain and are all individually decorated. The rooms feature a mixture of antique and modern furniture, some with wood burning stoves, others with deep freestanding pewter baths. One thing you can definitely expect from this location is a relaxing stay, outstanding service and delicious food. For those who like to get their hands dirty, Eckington Manor Cookery School offers a plethora of cookery courses to suit all capabilities. AGA cookery is a specialism at the school which boasts the largest number of AGAs in a UK cookery school.

Relish the region's exclusive offers.
See page 003 for details.

Judy Gardner, owner of Eckington Manor, has used the estate to bring her food ethos to life. The farm supplies the restaurant and cookery school with Highland and Aberdeen Angus beef and all other ingredients are sourced from local and trusted suppliers. The Restaurant at Eckington Manor honours the seasons with changing menus to reflect seasonal availability.

COTSWOLDS GOAT'S CHEESE & HAZELNUT TWICE COOKED SOUFFLE

SERVES 4

2010 Sancerre Les Boffants, Charles Dupuy, Loire Valley (France)

Ingredients

300ml milk
1 onion (sliced)
1 bay leaf
1 sprig fresh thyme
3 black peppercorns
30g butter
30g plain flour
45g Cerney goat's cheese
3 eggs (separated)
hazelnut oil
salt and pepper
hazelnut breadcrumbs

Garnish

grated parmesan
micro cress
roast tomatoes
sour cream and basil oil (to dress)

Method

For The Soufflé

Put the milk, sliced onion, bay leaf, thyme and black peppercorns into a saucepan then bring to a boil. Allow to infuse, then strain. In a separate pan, make a roux out of the butter and flour and slowly add the milk infusion a little at a time, until the mixture thickens. Add the cheese to the béchamel and, once melted, add the beaten egg yolks. Remove from the heat.

Beat the egg whites in a clean grease free bowl until stiff peaks are formed. Gently fold the egg whites into the béchamel in three stages and check seasoning.

Line four ramekins with hazelnut oil. Sprinkle a covering of hazelnut breadcrumbs, then top with the cheese mix to fill to two thirds of each ramekin. Bake in a *bain-marie* at 190°C for approximately 20 minutes or until risen and soft.

When cool turn out. When you are ready to serve, place the soufflés on a greased baking tray and put into a preheated oven at 230°C for five minutes.

Chef's Tip

However tempted you may be, do not open the oven whilst your soufflés are cooking or disaster will strike and they will sink!

To Serve

Glaze with grated parmesan and serve immediately. Plate as pictured and dress with a little sour cream and drizzle with drops of basil oil.

ECKINGTON BEEF STEAK SERVED WITH TRIPLE COOKED CHIPS & BEARNAISE SAUCE

SERVES 4

 2004 Senorio Amezola Reserva, Bodegas Amezola de la Mora, Rioja (Spain)

Ingredients

Steak

4 well marbled steaks (rib eye or sirloin)
4 plum tomatoes (eye removed and halved)
4 flat mushrooms
1 tbsp butter
salt and pepper
oil

Béarnaise Sauce

75g *clarified butter* (warm)
2 finely diced shallots
1 tsp peppercorns
3 tbsp white wine vinegar
3 tbsp dry white wine
2 tbsp tarragon and chervil (chopped)
3 egg yolks
1 tbsp cold water
salt and cayenne pepper (to taste)

Chips

potatoes
good vegetable oil
sea salt (to taste)

Method

For The Steak

The steak needs to be at room temperature before cooking.

Trim off any excess fat and heat a griddle pan or heavy frying pan. Brush the steak with a little oil and just before cooking, season with black pepper and salt. Grill the steak for two minutes on each side, then remove from the heat and rest for five minutes. Allowing the steak to rest at this time will reduce the amount of juices flowing out of the steak when cut.

Chef's Tip

We hang our beef for 30 days to ensure we get the best flavour and texture from the meat.

For The Tomatoes And Mushrooms

Whilst the steak is grilling, season the tomatoes and mushrooms, place the butter on top and cook alongside the steak. Continue to cook the mushrooms and tomatoes whilst the steak is resting.

For The Béarnaise Sauce

Place the tarragon, chervil and shallots in a small saucepan. In a mortar, crush the peppercorns and add to the pan. Cover with the white wine and white wine vinegar. Bring the mixture to a boil over a medium heat and reduce until the liquid has evaporated. Whisk the egg yolks and water over a *bain marie* until they are light and voluminous. Remove the bowl from the *bain marie* and slowly whisk in the *clarified butter*. Fold the shallot *reduction* into it, allow to cool then serve.

For The Chips

Chip potatoes into 2cm wide chips. *Blanch* in a pan of boiling, salted water for four to five minutes. Strain and dry off. Fry in a pan of oil in small batches until a light crust forms. Remove from the pan and place on kitchen towel to blot off some of the excess oil. Cool down in the fridge until ready to use. Heat the oil in a deep pan and fry your chips until golden brown for approximately seven minutes. Drain, blot with kitchen towel and sprinkle with sea salt.

To Serve

Serve as pictured.

ECKINGTON RHUBARB & RASPBERRY PAVLOVA

SERVES 6

🍷 *2008 Monbazillac Chateau Belingard*
(South West France)

Method

For The Meringues

Preheat the oven to 135°C and line a baking tray with greaseproof paper.

Meanwhile, put the egg whites and sugar in a pan and gently heat, stirring constantly until the sugar dissolves. Pour into a mixing bowl and whisk until you have soft peaks. Spoon onto the greaseproof paper in six mini pavlovas (tennis ball shape). Bake for 40 to 45 minutes until crunchy on the outside and soft inside.

Chef's Tip

Make sure all of your equipment is spotlessly clean and use a metal bowl to whisk your egg whites. Traces of oil can be difficult to remove from plastic bowls and will stop your whites from whisking properly.

For The Compôte

Chop fruit and add all the ingredients to a pan. Boil until fruit is softened.

To Serve

Add cream to a bowl and whisk until you have soft peaks. Slightly crush meringue on a plate, add a generous spoonful of the whipped cream, compôte, meringue crumbs and sauce.

Ingredients

Meringues

3 egg whites
175g caster sugar
white chocolate (to serve)

Compôte

1kg rhubarb
500g raspberries
sugar (to taste)
local honey (squeeze of)

600ml double cream

060
ELLENBOROUGH PARK

Southam Road, Cheltenham, Gloucestershire, GL52 3NJ

01242 545 454
www.ellenboroughpark.com

Since opening in March 2011, the 60-bedroomed Ellenborough Park has become Gloucestershire's first AA five star hotel and spa, achieved the Wine Spectator's 'Award of Excellence' two years in a row and named 'Hotel of the Year' 2012 Cotswold tourism awards. Quite some achievement for a new hotel. The interior appears as if from a bygone age. Walls draped with tapestries, classic furnishings from 1700 to 1800s and detail unrivalled amongst its peers. The nature of the building blends the old and new perfectly, with lots of nooks and crannies to enjoy a private meeting, a romantic drink, afternoon tea, or a read of the papers. The three AA Rosette Beaufort Dining Room is opulence personified. A relaxed, wood panelled interior, with wonderful light emanating through the stained glass windows overlooking Cheltenham Race Course in the distance, lends itself to chef David's beautifully created dishes.

Casual dining can also be enjoyed in The Brasserie, for more relaxed occasions. The informal, wooded bar-style venue is decorated in a sporting theme featuring the famous Cresta Run. Spa facilities are also on offer, with a pool (indoor and out), sauna and seven treatment rooms. All in all it makes Ellenborough Park the perfect location to explore Cheltenham and the surrounding Cotswolds. No need to bring your wellies, they have a rather impressive 'boot room' worth a visit.

Relish the region's exclusive offers.
See page 003 for details.

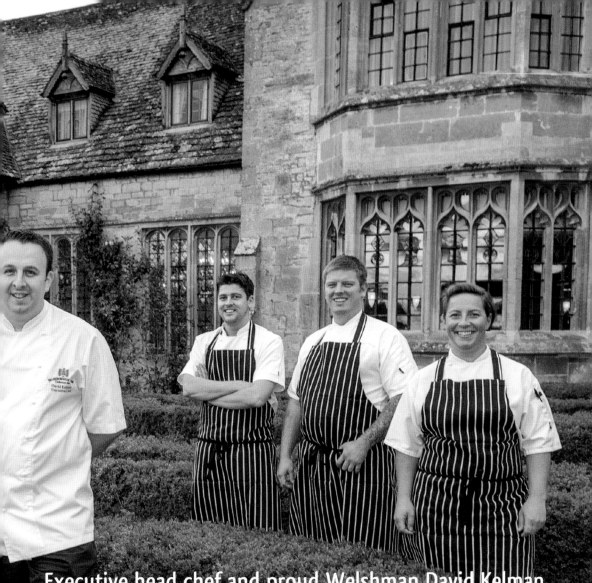

Executive head chef and proud Welshman David Kelman has not only managed to achieve three AA Rosettes for The Beaufort Dining Room but he has also represented his country in many international culinary competitions and been privileged to cook for Her Majesty the Queen and HRH the Prince of Wales. David is a stalwart of the region having previously worked at Lower Slaughter Manor, where he also gained three AA rosettes for food, contributing to the hotel's accolade of becoming a Relais & Chateau member

BOILED ORGANIC EGG & SOLDIERS WITH ENGLISH ASPARAGUS & CRISP OXSPRINGS AIR-DRIED HAM

SERVES 4

 Yealands Estate Gruner Veltliner, Black label, Awatere Valley, 2011 (New Zealand)

Ingredients

Eggs
4 organic eggs
4 tbsp mayonnaise

Breadsticks
4 slices white or brown bread
1 clove garlic (sliced)
100ml olive oil

16 spears asparagus (peeled and cut into 7^1/2cm pieces)

4 slices Oxsprings air-dried ham

Garnish
4 red radishes
1 packet edible flowers (optional)
1 bunch watercress
100g peas (shelled and cooked)

Method

For The Eggs
With a sharp knife or egg topper remove the top of the eggs.

Carefully pour the egg from the shells and poach until they're a little soft in the centre. Place into cold water to chill.

Place the shells into a pan of boiling salted water to clean and with your finger remove the membrane from within each shell. Dry and put to one side.

For the filling, place the poached eggs into a blender with the mayonnaise and blend until thick.

Season and place into a container.

For The Breadsticks
Remove the crusts then cut the bread into four equal sized sticks.

Drizzle with the olive oil and add a few slices of garlic to the tray.

Bake at 160°C until crisp and golden brown.

Remove from the oven and cool.

For The Asparagus
Blanch the asparagus in a pan of boiling, salted water for one minute. Refresh in cold running water.

For The Air-dried Ham
Lay the slices of ham on a baking tray and place into the oven at 160°C until crisp.

Remove from the oven and leave to cool.

To Serve
In the bottom of the four egg shells, place an equal amount of peas and watercress.

Spoon the egg mixture into the shells until full. Smooth flat with a knife.

Place each egg into an egg cup on a plate. At the base of the egg cup arrange the asparagus, breadstick, edible flowers, watercress and crisp air-dried ham. Complete with a scattering of radishes.

ROAST FILLET OF COD WITH WARM SALAD OF BABY VEGETABLES, SAFFRON TURNED POTATOES & TOMATO DRESSING

SERVES 4

 Chassagne Montrachet, Bernard Moreau 2010 (France)

Ingredients

Cod

centre cut cod fillet from a 2kg plus sized fish

Tomato Dressing

4 baby plum or cherry tomatoes
200ml light olive oil
1 clove garlic (sliced)

Saffron Potatoes

8 large new potatoes
1 clove garlic (sliced)
saffron

Cherry Tomatoes

10 baby plum or cherry tomatoes
light olive oil
salt and pepper

4 spears asparagus (peeled and *blanched*)
6 baby fennel (cooked and pulled apart)
8 baby carrots (peeled and cooked)
4 baby beetroot (peeled and cooked)
200g baby spinach
10g butter (for vegetables)

soft butter (to brush plate)
beetroot powder

Method

To Prepare The Cod

Trim the cod fillet into a neat, long even piece.

Lightly salt the fish, roll tightly in clingfilm and place in the fridge for six hours. Remove from the fridge, wash the salt off and re-roll in clingfilm. Cut into four equal pieces.

For The Tomato Dressing

Warm the oil with the garlic in a pan.

Place the tomatoes into a blender and blend until they are broken down. Slowly pour the garlic infused oil into the tomatoes as the blender is still going - this will *emulsify*. When thick and smooth, remove from the blender and place into a container.

For The Saffron Potatoes

Peel the potatoes. Using a knife, trim into a barrel shape.

Place into a pan of cold water with the garlic and a pinch of saffron and salt. Cook until soft, then chill over cold water.

For The Cherry Tomatoes

Slice the tomatoes in half and season. Drizzle with a little olive oil and place into a warm, low oven and leave for about six hours until soft.

For The Cod

Remove the cod from the clingfilm and with a hot non-stick pan, add a little oil and place the cod skin side down into the pan. When you have some colour on the skin, turn the gas/electric down to low and leave for five minutes. Turn the fish and cook on the other side for a further four to five minutes, until cooked.

With a pastry brush, lightly brush the softened butter over the plate and dust with the beetroot powder. Shake off any excess powder (see picture).

To Assemble And Serve

In a warm pan, wilt the spinach and season. Dry in a cloth so no excess juices leak onto the plate.

Warm the potatoes and vegetables in a pan - make sure the beetroot is warmed up in a different pan so that it does not bleed onto the vegetables. Season and add a little butter.

Place a small amount of spinach in the middle of the plate then arrange the cod on top.

Dress the plate with the tomatoes, vegetables and potatoes as pictured. Drizzle some of the tomato dressing around the plate.

GINGER BRANDY SNAP FILLED WITH RHUBARB MASCARPONE, GINGER SET CREAM, POACHED RHUBARB & A YOGHURT SORBET

SERVES 4

🍷 *Peller Estate Ice Cuvee Classic, Niagara Peninsula, NV (Non Vintage), (Canada)*

Ingredients

Brandy Snap

100g soft unsalted butter
90g golden syrup
180g caster sugar
90g plain flour
$^1/_2$ tsp ground ginger

Poached Rhubarb

100g sugar
2 fat sticks rhubarb
100ml grenadine
200ml water

Ginger Set Cream

200ml double cream
200ml milk
4g agar agar
100g caster sugar
$^1/_2$ tsp ground ginger

Yoghurt Sorbet

375g caster sugar
568ml water
500g Greek yoghurt
1 drop vanilla essence

Mascarpone

200g mascarpone
100g rhubarb trimmings (chopped - from the poached rhubarb)

Chef's Tip

Garnish with a toffee sauce and sliced, poached rhubarb.

Method

For The Brandy Snap

Put all the ingredients into a blender and blend until all the ingredients are mixed well. Place in the fridge for approximately four hours. Once chilled, roll into 12g balls. Place onto a tray lined with greaseproof paper and bake at 170°C until light brown in colour. Remove from the oven and place another sheet of greaseproof paper on top and, using a rolling pin, roll really flat.

Leave to cool, then remove the paper. Place back into the oven to gently warm the brandy snaps then cut into a rectangular shape whilst still soft and bend around a pipe. Cool and remove from the pipe. Store in an air tight container until required.

For The Sorbet

Put the sugar and water into a pan and bring to a boil and simmer for two to five minutes. Cool down. When cold, mix 500ml of the syrup into 500g of the yoghurt and add a little of vanilla essence. Place into an ice cream machine and churn until frozen.

For The Poached Rhubarb

Put the water, grenadine and sugar into a pan and bring to a boil. Add the rhubarb and simmer until soft. Chill in the fridge for two hours or until cold.

Remove from the fridge and cut into 2.5cm lengths - keeping some extra slices for the plate. Retain all the trimmings for the mascarpone mix.

For The Ginger Set Cream

In a pan, bring the milk, cream, ginger and sugar to a boil. Add the agar agar to the hot liquid then re-boil - make sure the liquid boils so it activates the agar agar.

Pour the liquid into a small rectangle tray (approximately 200mm x 100mm x 30mm deep) lined with greaseproof paper and place in the fridge to set.

Mascarpone

Mix together the mascarpone and poached rhubarb trimmings.

To Serve

Using a cutter, cut a round shape out of the ginger set cream. Pipe some of the mascarpone mix into the brandy tube - fill to the top. Place the tube next to the set cream. Spoon the rhubarb onto the set cream. Dress the plate with toffee sauce (optional), sliced poached rhubarb and a scoop of yoghurt sorbet.

070
THE FEATHERED NEST COUNTRY INN

Nether Westcote, Oxfordshire, OX7 6SD

01993 833 030
www.thefeatherednestinn.co.uk

Since Amanda and Tony Timmer bought the previously neglected Inn, it has undergone a transformation like no other. A top to toe restoration included beams being brought down from a monastery in Manchester, artefacts from all over the world and the sort of attention to detail that one would expect from a top surgeon and not necessarily from a restaurateur. The results are an immaculate example of the 'perfect English country pub' complete with bar stools made from saddles.

Supported by their loyal customers from all over the world, the couple have earned a string of awards including AA Pub of the Year 2011/12, Beautiful South Pub of the Year 2012/2013, Good Hotel Guide César Award 2013 and topped in January 2013 by achieving three AA Rosettes for the cuisine created by chef Kuba Winkowski and his dedicated brigade. Born in Poland, chef Kuba says his passions for depth of flavour and detailed presentation is down to his poor food selection during his upbringing - he wanted to 'bring colour into his food.'

'The Nest', set in 45 acres of land, provides a herb and vegetable garden, game for the larder, and allows the kitchen brigade to forage for seasonal produce.

It is advisable to visit as soon as possible before everyone discovers this stunning example of a classic English country pub, set in one of the most picturesque Cotswold settings.

Relish the region's exclusive offers.
See page 003 for details.

Owners, Tony and Amanda, have created the perfect mix at The Feathered Nest Inn. With Tony's passion for perfection driven by his vision to create the 'perfect English country pub', Amanda's attention to detail and experience as an interior designer, along with chef Kuba's constant drive to create the perfect dish, utilising the ingredients from the surrounding region - instilled in him from his days spent at Le Manoir - The Feathered Nest has all the ingredients for the perfect country pub experience.

BAKED CORNISH RED MULLET WITH ARTICHOKES

SERVES 4

 Charles Melton 'Rose of Virginia', 2011 (Australia)

Ingredients

2 x 250g Cornish red mullets

Broth

8 baby globe artichokes
100ml extra virgin olive oil
100g onions
150g carrots
100g fennel
100g celery
50g smoked streaky bacon lardons
300ml chicken stock
150ml white wine
20ml lemon juice
5g salt
1 bay leaf
1 sprig thyme
2 garlic cloves

Croutons

1 bread roll
20ml olive oil
1 garlic clove

Garnish

4 caper berries

50g black olive tapenade (available in most speciality food shops)
fennel tops

Method

For The Mullet

Remove the scales. Fillet and pin bone the red mullet or ask your fishmonger to do it for you. Place skin side down on oiled baking paper in an oven tray. Reserve for later.

For The Broth

Wash, peel and dice all the vegetables into medium size cubes - apart from the artichoke.

Pull off the outer leaves of the baby artichokes until you reach leaves that are mostly yellow. Cut the top part of the leaves and discard. Finish trimming any green leaves off the stem.
Leave the heart intact with the stem (4cm long) and peel with a vegetable peeler. Cut the artichokes in half and remove any furry bits from the middle. Place in lemon water while preparing the rest.

In a heavy bottomed pan, on a medium heat, cook bacon in olive oil for three minutes. Add all the diced vegetables, prepared artichokes, salt, bay leaf, thyme and sliced garlic and sweat them under the lid for five minutes.

Separately boil the white wine for two minutes. Add the boiled wine, lemon juice and stock to the artichokes, in a pan, and simmer until the artichokes are soft and tender, but not mushy.

When ready, take out 12 pieces of artichokes and one third of the vegetables out of the broth and keep for garnishing.

Liquidise the rest of the broth and pass through a sieve. Check seasoning.

For The Croutons

Preheat oven to 160°C. Slice the bread roll as thinly as possible and drizzle with olive oil. Bake in the oven until golden. When ready, brush with half a garlic clove.

To Serve

Season the red mullet and bake for five to six minutes.

Place reserved vegetables and artichokes in the serving bowl. Arrange croutons, pour the broth, place baked red mullet and garnish with caper berries, black olive tapenade and fennel tops.

ROASTED FREE RANGE COTSWOLD CHICKEN BREAST, LIVER & ONION TART

SERVES 4

 *Huia Pinot Noir, 2010*
(New Zealand)

Ingredients

4 x Cotswold White free range chicken breasts
100g chicken hearts

Tart

all butter ready rolled puff pastry
300g onions
20g butter
100g chicken livers
50g smoked bacon lardons
150g Savoy cabbage
9cm disc cutter

Garnish

12 baby turnips
12 baby carrots
20g butter
1 sprig thyme

Purée

300g swede
20g butter
300ml water

Thyme Foam

500ml milk
6 gelatine leaves
30g thyme

Sauce

30g butter
100g shallots
100g button mushrooms
30g plain flour
500ml chicken stock, 100ml red wine

Method

For The Tart

Finely slice onions and caramelise them slowly in butter until golden brown. Leave to cool. Chop chicken livers to almost a purée and mix with onion. Season with salt and pepper to taste.

Cut out four 8cm disks of puff pastry, place them between two baking sheets and bake at 180°C for about ten minutes until golden brown. Let them cool down. Spread onion and liver mix on the tarts and reserve for later.

For The Tart Filling

Slice cabbage into fine strips and *blanch* in boiling, salted water for four minutes and refresh in ice water. Meanwhile cook bacon lardons in a little oil for two minutes, put aside and mix in the drained cabbage when cold.

For The Garnish

Bring 300ml of water to a boil with the butter, thyme sprig and a good pinch of salt. *Blanch* baby turnips and carrots until tender and refresh in ice water. When cold remove the skin and trim the green tops to 1cm.

For The Purée

Peel and dice the swede into small cubes, add the butter and a pinch of salt. Cook, with a lid on the pan, until mushy then purée.

For The Foam

Place milk and thyme in a saucepan and bring to a boil. Take off the heat and infuse for two hours. Pass through a fine sieve.

Soak gelatine in cold water. Bring infused milk to a simmer and dissolve the soaked gelatine. Keep warm and reserve for later.

For The Sauce

In a saucepan, reduce red wine by half and set aside. Caramelise shallots and mushrooms in the butter until golden brown and crispy. Add flour and cook for three minutes. Add reduced red wine and stock. Stir until thickened and cook for ten minutes on a low heat. Pass through a fine sieve.

To Serve

While the chicken is resting, cook the tart in the oven for six to eight minutes. Panfry the chicken hearts in butter for five minutes until nicely coloured and tender. Do not overcook.

Warm up the cabbage, turnips, carrots and swede purée.

On a large plate, place dots of swede purée, turnips and carrots. Place the tart in the middle and top with bacon cabbage. Slice the chicken breasts into five pieces and stack up on the tart. Pour sauce around the tart and dot frothed up foam (use a milk frother or hand blender).

POACHED RHUBARB, SORBET, & YOGHURT SAUCE, PISTACHIO CRUMBLE & OLIVE OIL CAKE

SERVES 4

 *Vin de Constance, 2010
(South Africa)*

Ingredients

Poached Rhubarb

500g rhubarb (cut into 4cm long sticks)
50g caster sugar
250ml orange juice
100g caster sugar

Poached Sorbet

50ml cold water
450g rhubarb
100g caster sugar

Olive Oil Cake

50g fine polenta
200g ground pistachios
50g plain flour
1 tsp baking powder
65ml olive oil
100g butter
3 eggs (at room temperature)
200g caster sugar
1 lemon (juice and zest)
1 orange (juice)

Pistachio Crumble

110g butter (softened)
110g demerara sugar
200g plain flour
100g ground pistachios

Yoghurt Sauce

200g natural yoghurt
1 vanilla pod (seeds)
30g sugar

Yoghurt Tuile (optional)

125g fondant
65g glucose
65g Isomalt
50g Yopol, yoghurt powder

Method

For The Poached Rhubarb

Marinate the rhubarb sticks for two hours with the 50g of sugar. Heat the orange juice with the 100g of sugar, pour over the rhubarb in a flat tray. Cover tightly with foil and cook in the oven at 160°C for about 25 minutes until tender. Cool, cover with foil and reserve in fridge until needed. Reduce some of the juice to a sticky syrup for garnish.

For The Rhubarb Sorbet

Place the water, rhubarb and sugar into a pan, cover with a lid and bring to a boil for two to three minutes. Remove the lid, reduce the heat and simmer for a further four to five minutes until the rhubarb is tender. Set aside to cool then blend to a purée in a food processor. Pass the puréed rhubarb through a fine sieve, check sweetness and add more sugar if necessary. Churn in an ice cream maker, following the manufacturer's instructions, until the sorbet is smooth and has set. Store in the freezer until needed.

For The Olive Oil Cake

Whisk the eggs and caster sugar until pale and fluffy. Mix the polenta, ground pistachios, flour and baking powder together. Melt butter and mix with olive oil. Whisk the butter and olive oil in to the eggs and sugar and add polenta and pistachio mix. Add zest and juices and mix gently. Pour into a greased 20cm cake tin and cook at 160°C for 30 minutes. Cool. Trim the brown edges to expose green cake. Cut into 4cm long and 2cm high rectangles.

For The Pistachio Crumble

Rub the butter into the flour and sugar. Add a few drops of water and mix to create medium size lumps. Place on a baking sheet and bake until golden brown at 180°C for about ten minutes. When cold, mix with ground pistachios.

For The Yoghurt Sauce

Mix together the natural yoghurt, vanilla seeds and sugar.

For The Yoghurt Tuile

Put the fondant and the glucose in a pan and stir until dissolved. Add the Isomalt at 115°C. Cook on medium heat until the thermometer reaches 160°C (it will reach the missing 5°C with its own heat). Take off the heat and cool to 140°C. Add yoghurt powder, stirring constantly. Spread on a 'bake-o-glide' sheet and when cold, blitz in a blender to a fine powder. With a sieve, sprinkle powder onto a piece of greaseproof paper. Place in the oven at 170°C for one to two minutes. Once melted and crunchy, leave to cool and keep in a sealed container in a cool, dry place.

To Serve

Warm up the pistachio cake and plate as pictured.

080
THE KING'S HEAD INN

The Green, Bledington, Oxfordshire, OX7 6XQ

01608 658 365
www.thekingsheadinn.net

Originally built as a cider house, The King's Head Inn is in one of the Cotswolds most beautiful pubs. Dating back to the 16th Century, it has been lovingly restored and improved by private owners Archie and Nicola Orr-Ewing.

They have transformed the venue during the past 12 years and today customers can look forward to open fires in winter or a gloriously picturesque village green in Summer. The setting is idyllic - ducks and bantams wander freely around the grounds.

The Inn benefits from 12 elegant bedrooms some of which have exposed beams or overlook the adjacent brook, or the pretty courtyard garden. Artfully decorated and inspired by chic, funky style, they provide the perfect base for those looking to explore. It also features in the Michelin Pub Guide, The Good Food Guide and was the cover star for The Good Pub Guide 2012.

Matt Laughton, head chef, who also oversees The Swan Inn at Swinbrook, has great links with local suppliers, who provide him with the best of Cotswold flavour. "We've got an unimaginably good larder right here on our doorstep," he says. "It's a real privilege to have such good connections with the local food and farming community. We get the best produce delivered straight to the kitchen. We believe in classical flavours, where great ingredients are left to do the talking.

"We always try to use as much free-range, organic and local produce as we possibly can when making our dishes. Our beef, which is Aberdeen Angus, is sourced locally from the family farm in Fifield. Our fish is delivered daily from Cornwall and all our smoked food is from Upton Smokery in Burford."

Wendnesday Burger Night

ALL ~ £10

* Chicken fillet burger with bacon & cheese
* Chilli Cheeseburger, harissa mayonnaise
* Roe deer & blue cheese burger

Dating back to the 16th Century, The King's Head Inn has been lovingly restored and improved by private owners Archie and Nicola Orr-Ewing.

SEARED SCOTTISH SCALLOPS, CRISP TAMWORTH BELLY PORK, PICCALILLI & APPLE PUREE

SERVES 4

 Riesling, Reichsrat von Buhl 2011 (Germany)

Ingredients

200g slow cooked pork belly

Scallops

12 Scottish scallops (roe removed)
$^1/_4$ lemon (juiced)
25g butter

Apple Purée

1 large Cox's Apple Pippin apple
10g sugar
5g butter
$^1/_4$ lemon (juiced)

Piccalilli

75g sea salt
$^3/_4$ ltr water
50g carrot (diced)
50g cucumber (diced)
50g cauliflower (small florets)
50g red pepper (diced and skinned)
25g red chilli (finely diced)
25g shallot (diced)
250ml cider vinegar
$^1/_2$ star anise
5 peppercorns
1 bay leaf
$^1/_4$ tsp turmeric
$^1/_2$ tsp ground ginger
1 tsp mustard powder
10g plain flour

Garnish

micro cress

Method

For The Pork Belly

Place a wire rack on a deep roasting tray. Add just enough water to touch the top of the wire rack. Wrap the tray in foil and cook at 150°C for approximately two to three hours or until tender. Remove from the tray, press and cool. When chilled, cut into 2cm squares and set aside.

For The Piccalilli (Prepare the day before)

Start by warming the water to 37°C. Dissolve the sea salt in the water to create a brine. Pour over the chopped vegetables and leave overnight. (This will draw out any unwanted moisture to give a nice crisp piccalilli).

Place the vinegar, bay leaf, star anise and peppercorns into a saucepan, cover and slowly warm.

In a separate bowl, mix the mustard powder, turmeric, ginger and plain flour. Add a splash of vinegar to help create a smooth paste. Next, strain over the vinegar mixture and return to the pan over a medium heat. Cook for five to ten minutes, stirring constantly to avoid going lumpy.

Strain the vegetables, but do not rinse. Add to vinegar mixture and cook for one minute. Use chilli as you require. Set aside and chill.

For The Apple Purée

Place all ingredients in a saucepan and cook until the apples are tender, then purée.

To Serve

Sear the scallops in a non stick frying pan over a medium high heat for one to two minutes. When they have caramelised, turn over and remove from the heat. Add the butter and lemon juice. Remove from the pan and rest.

Crisp the pork belly under a hot grill until golden nutty brown.

Serve as required with the apple purée and chilled piccalilli.

Chef's Tip

Don't season the scallops until cooked as this will start to draw out the moisture.

HERB CRUSTED RACK OF COTSWOLD LAMB, CELERIAC, WATERCRESS PESTO & OYSTER MUSHROOMS

SERVES 4

 Château des Gravieres Collection Prestige, Graves 2009 (France)

Ingredients

2 x 6 bone racks of Cotswold lamb (scarred on skin side and seasoned with salt and pepper)

Herb Crumb

100g fresh breadcrumbs
$^1/_2$ tsp chopped mint
$^1/_2$ tsp flat leaf parsley (chopped)
$^1/_2$ tsp rosemary (chopped)
1 clove garlic (chopped)
25ml rapeseed oil
2g Maldon sea salt
$^1/_4$ tsp ground black pepper

Watercress Pesto

200g fresh watercress (washed)
1 clove garlic
25g Double Gloucester cheese (grated)
10g pinenuts
$^1/_2$ lemon (juice)
100ml extra virgin olive oil

oyster mushrooms (lightly sautéed)
celeriac (braised)

Method

For The Herb Crumb

Place all dry ingredients in a food processor and blitz until all ingredients are mixed. Add enough oil just to bind.

For The Lamb

Remove the lamb from the fridge 30 minutes before cooking to allow the meat to cook more evenly. Season.

Sear in a hot pan to help retain the lamb's natural juices, then allow to rest for ten minutes. Cover with the herb crumb and place in the oven at 200°C for approximately six to eight minutes for medium rare. Adjust cooking times to suit. When cooked, lightly cover with foil and allow to rest for another six to eight minutes.

For The Watercress Pesto

Liquidise all the ingredients until smooth - season to taste.

To Serve

When the lamb has rested, serve on the watercress pesto, braised celeriac and oyster mushrooms.

> **Chef's Tip**
> Use bread two to three days old to keep the crumbs nice and crisp.

PERRY POACHED PEAR TART, PRALINE CREAM, POMEGRANATE & CITRUS SALSA

SERVES 4

🍷 *Aleatico di Puglia, Francesco Candido 2003
(Italy)*

Ingredients

Tart
4 x 6 cm round of ready rolled puff pastry
1 egg yolk (beaten)
demerara sugar

Pears
4 x ripe Williams pears
200ml perry
200g caster sugar
1 kafir lime leaf
$1/2$ star anise

Praline Cream
100ml double cream
1 tsp praline

Salsa
1 orange (zest and segmented)
1 lime (zest and segmented)
1 lemon (zest and segmented)
4 sprigs of mint (finely chopped)

Garnish
$1/2$ pomegranate (fruit only)

Method

For The Tart
Brush the puff pastry rounds with the beaten egg yolk. Sprinkle with demerara sugar and cook in a preheated oven at 220°C for eight to ten minutes or until evenly golden brown. Remove to rack and cool.

For The Pears
Peel the pears and place in lightly *acidulated* water. Place all other ingredients in a saucepan and bring to a boil. When liquid is boiling, move to a low heat and add the pears to cook until just tender. Remove the pears to cool and save the liquid for later.

For The Praline Cream
Whisk all the ingredients to form soft peaks. Set aside.

For The Salsa
Reduce the poaching liquor over a medium high heat and reduce by half. Remove from the heat and chill. When cool, add all the remaining ingredients.

To Serve
Place the tart base on a plate then pipe or spoon on the praline cream. Top with the poached pears, drizzle on the salsa and sprinkle the pomegranate seeds around.

Chef's Tip
Use unwaxed citrus fruits.

090
LE MANOIR AUX QUAT'SAISONS

Church Road, Great Milton, Oxford, OX44 7PD

0184 427 8881
www.manoir.com

The modern French menu at Raymond Blanc's two Michelin starred Le Manoir aux Quat'Saisons restaurant has been described as "a twist of imaginative genius" and the cuisine is undoubtedly the focus of every guest's visit.

The quality of the food stems from the freshness and purity of its ingredients. The two acre kitchen garden produces 90 types of vegetables and over 70 varieties of herbs. Raymond Blanc has been a champion of the organic movement for the last 28 years and says, "Flavour alone would be a reason to buy organic food, quite apart from its freedom from additives."

His executive head chef since 1999 is Gary Jones, whom Raymond describes as "the most gifted chef I know." He also wrote the foreword to this book and helps to train many of the acclaimed chefs within.

Complementing the menus is a superb range of wines. Le Manoir's wine cellar, which nestles beneath the conservatory, is home to around 1,000 different wines from around the world, with around 60% being of French provenance.

The Raymond Blanc Cookery School at Le Manoir aux Quat'Saisons attracts people from around the world. The word used most often by the cookery school students to describe their experience is "fun" and that is what the school is all about. It offers people with a passion for food the skills to prepare fantastic dishes and have a great time while doing so.

During a one, two, or four day course anyone from a complete novice to an accomplished enthusiast can learn the secrets of producing fine food. Tuition by Le Manoir's expert cookery school chefs is led by head tutor Mark Peregrine, who brings over 30 years of experience to the role.

Naturally, in addition to the hands-on learning experience, students benefit from a luxurious break in the enchanting surroundings of Le Manoir and the chance to meet new friends.

Relish the region's exclusive offers.
See page 003 for details.

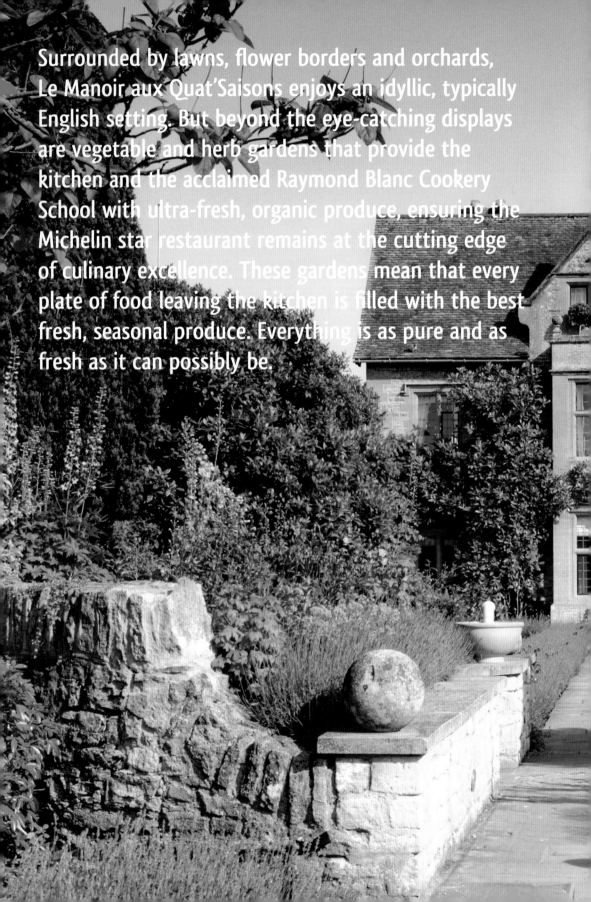

Surrounded by lawns, flower borders and orchards, Le Manoir aux Quat'Saisons enjoys an idyllic, typically English setting. But beyond the eye-catching displays are vegetable and herb gardens that provide the kitchen and the acclaimed Raymond Blanc Cookery School with ultra-fresh, organic produce, ensuring the Michelin star restaurant remains at the cutting edge of culinary excellence. These gardens mean that every plate of food leaving the kitchen is filled with the best fresh, seasonal produce. Everything is as pure and as fresh as it can possibly be.

GARDEN BEETS, HORSERADISH & DILL

SERVES 8

 Ménetou-Salon Moroques 2010, Henri Pellé
(Loire, France)

Ingredients

Baby Beets (makes approx 500g)

10 baby beetroots
1g salt
0.15g ground black pepper
5ml Cabernet Sauvignon vinegar
$^1/_2$g caster sugar
10ml early harvest cooking olive oil

Beetroot And Horseradish Sorbet
(makes approx 500g)

50ml liquid glucose
500ml golden beetroot juice
2g of vitamin C powder (which should be mixed
with the beetroot juice)
28g creamed horseradish
3g salt

Beetroot Terrine And Glaze
(makes 1 x 600g terrine)

400ml beetroot juice (reduced to 200ml)
375ml Sandermans ruby port (reduced to 180ml)
22ml Cabernet Sauvignon vinegar (boiled)
25ml aged balsamic vinegar (8 years old)
4g salt
0.1g ground black pepper
3.75g agar agar
250g ruby beetroot (cooked, sliced and trimmed
for the terrine mould)

Horseradish Cream

130g creamed horseradish
90g crème fraîche
4g salt
3g caster sugar
5ml lemon juice
$^1/_2$g cayenne pepper

Garnish

beetroot carpaccio
fresh dill
baby beetroot
beetroot and horseradish sorbet
horseradish cream

Method

For The Accomplished Chef!

Our garden beetroot layered into a terrine and set with
agar agar. Garnished with horseradish cream, garden beetroot,
golden beetroot and horseradish sorbet.

For The Baby Beets

Wash the baby beetroots to remove any soil or dirt. Sort the
beetroots into sizes - small, medium and large. Steam the beetroots
for around 40 minutes, until tender. The smaller beetroots will
steam more quickly than the large. When chilled, peel the outer
skin and portion. Dress the beetroots with salt, pepper, sugar, olive
oil and Cabernet Sauvignon vinegar, as required.

For The Beetroot And Horseradish Sorbet

In a heavy bottomed pan, warm the glucose liquid. Once warm,
remove from the stove and add remaining ingredients.
Mix together well and adjust the seasoning. Pass through a fine
chinois. Chill and churn in an ice cream machine. Churn and
quenelle before serving.

For The Terrine And Glaze

To Make The Jelly
Reduce the port by half. Reduce the beetroot juice by half.
Bring the Cabernet Sauvignon vinegar to a boil and add to the
port and beetroot reductions. Take a third of this liquid and bring
to a simmer with the agar agar and cook for five minutes,
whisking constantly. Remove from the heat once the agar agar
has dissolved. Add the remaining liquid, balsamic, salt and
pepper to taste. Pour the first layer of beetroot jelly into the
terrine mould 6mm thick. Add trimmed, cooked beetroots then
add another layer of beetroot jelly. Beets, jelly, beets then jelly.
It will set rapidly. Ensure the last layer of jelly covers the beets by
6mm. Retain a small amount of jelly for the glaze.

To Make The Glaze
Liquidise the remaining jelly and pass through a muslin cloth.

For The Horseradish Cream

Liquidise all ingredients until smooth. Pass through a *chinois*.
Season to taste.

To Serve

Slice the beetroot terrine into eight 60g to 70g portions and
place on the plate with the glaze. Decorate with three baby
beets, a quenelle of horseradish cream, beetroot and horseradish
sorbet, beetroot carpaccio and fresh dill.

TURBOT, NATIVE OYSTER & SCALLOP, CUCUMBER & WASABI

SERVES 1 (per person)

 Meursault Les Chevalières 2002, Jean-Philippe Fichet (Bourgogne, France)

Ingredients

90g turbot
1 native Cornish assured oyster
30ml lemongrass braisage (to cook the fish)
12g cucumber ribbons
1/2 hand-dived scallop (medium)

Cucumber And Wasabi Beurre Blanc
(makes 200g)

60g sliced banana shallot
80g cucumber flesh
60ml Chardonnay
50ml white wine vinegar
50ml whipping cream
50ml water
170g unsalted butter (cold)
70g cucumber skin, 20g wasabi paste
1/2ml lemon juice, 1.25g salt
pinch cayenne pepper

Lemongrass Braisage (makes 200ml)

50g sliced shallot, 10g unsalted butter
pinch of salt
125g button mushrooms
150ml Chardonnay, 100ml Noilly Prat
20g fresh lemongrass (smashed then finely
chopped)
100ml double cream
150g turbot bones
50g unsalted butter (cold, to finish)
7ml lemon juice, pinch cayenne pepper

Wasabi Foam (makes 380g)

200ml lemongrass braisage
60g cucumber skin, 12g wasabi paste
1g lecite, 1g salt, 1ml lemon juice

To Serve

12g pak choi (wilted)
14g baby spinach (wilted)
1g micro herbs
2g wasabi foam (see below)
2g mixed seaweed, 2g Osietra caviar
30g cucumber and wasabi *beurre blanc*

Method

For The Accomplished Chef!

For The Turbot

Cook the turbot in the braisage in a covered pan at 55°C for ten minutes. After six minutes, add the scallops to the braisage and warm to 55°C. Reserve some braisage for the wasabi foam. Do not allow to simmer. Cook the oyster in its own juice and warm the cucumber ribbons in the same pan. They should both reach 55°C.

For The Cucumber And Wasabi Beurre Blanc

Put the shallot, cucumber flesh, white wine and white wine vinegar into a pan. Reduce until all liquid is gone. Do not caramelise or catch pan. Rest pan to ensure maximum evaporation. Add cream and a dash of water. Bring to a boil. Gradually whisk in cold butter until fully incorporated, then pass through a *chinois*. Add cucumber skins and wasabi. Liquidise until green. Pass through *chinois*. Add salt, cayenne and lemon to taste.

> **Chef's Tip**
>
> The cucumber and wasabi *beurre blanc* can be enhanced with the juice of an oyster.

For The Lemongrass Braisage

Sweat shallots in butter until very soft with a pinch of salt. Do not colour. Add sliced mushrooms and stir over a medium heat. Cover with clingfilm until they give up their juices. Do not at any stage caramelise the mixture in the pan. Add Chardonnay and reduce by half. Now add Noilly Prat, lemongrass, cream and fish bones. Bring to a boil rapidly in a heavy bottomed pan for six minutes. Pass through a fine *chinois* to extract maximum juice and flavour from ingredients. Whisk in butter and lemon juice and a little salt and cayenne to taste. All butter should dissolve.

For The Wasabi Foam

Warm the braisage, blitz ingredients and pass through a fine *chinois*. Chill until required. Then, liquidise and take the foam from the top, or, alternatively, use a hand blender.

To Serve

Place the wilted spinach and pak choi in the bottom of the bowl. Place the fish in the centre of the bowl. Place the cucumber, seaweed and oyster on top of the turbot. Finish with the wasabi *beurre blanc*, caviar and micro herbs. Spoon over a little wasabi foam.

MULLED WINTER FRUITS, CINNAMON ICE CREAM

SERVES 4

🍷 *Otima Tawny Port 10 Year Old (served chilled) (Portugal)*

Ingredients

Poaching Liquor

500ml red wine (reduced to 250ml)
150ml Sandermans ruby port (brought to a boil)
4 whole cloves
1 star anise
$\frac{1}{2}$g orange zest, $\frac{1}{2}$g lemon zest
1 six inch cinnamon stick
6 black peppercorns
20g muscavado sugar
60ml orange juice
100ml black cherry purée

Fruit

280g Cox's Orange Pippin apples (approximately two cut into quarters)
280g Williams pears (approximately two, cut into quarters)
4 fresh figs (cut into quarters)
2 plums (cut into six)

Cinnamon Ice Cream (makes 2.7 ltrs)

21 cinnamon sticks
2 ltr full fat milk, 330g caster sugar
20ml hot water
400g egg yolk
170g caster sugar
40g Suprema milk powder
40g Diamante 50 (stabiliser)

Pain d'Epices (makes 510g)

160g free range eggs
48g caster sugar
2g five spice powder, 3.2g vanilla extract
$\frac{1}{2}$g orange zest
120ml full fat milk (warmed)
240g heather blossom honey
160g flour (rye t170 viron), 80g plain flour
16g baking powder
30g *clarified butter,* 250g caster sugar (to glaze)

To Serve

15g pain d'Epices
40g cinnamon ice cream

Method

For The Accomplished Chef!

For The Poaching Liquor

Reduce red wine by half. Bring port to a boil. Tie the aromats in a muslin cloth (star anise, zests, cinnamon sticks, black peppercorns, cloves). Add orange juice and sugar to the alcohols and infuse aromats. Add cherry purée.

For The Fruit (Prepare the day before)

Gently poach the fruit in the liquor, until just cooked. Place in a kilner jar and allow to chill overnight.

For The Ice Cream

Roast the cinnamon sticks in the oven for five to six minutes at 140°C, then gently break into pieces. Bring the milk to a boil and infuse the roasted cinnamon for 30 minutes. Bring the 330g of caster sugar to a brown caramel. Take off the gas and add in 20ml of hot water to stop the cooking. Then, whisk in the carefully strained milk infusion. Whisk the egg yolks with a little infused milk and 170g caster sugar, dried milk and stabiliser. *Pasteurise* up to 85°C then allow to cool to 4°C. Pass through a *chinois*. Churn in ice cream machine and freeze until required.

For The Pain d'Epices

In a bowl, lightly mix the eggs and caster sugar. Add the five spice, vanilla extract and orange zest. Add in the warmed milk and honey, bring to 45°C. Fold the flour into the mix. Spread onto a non-stick mat and cook for six to seven minutes at 170°C.

In a pan, caramelise 30g *clarified butter* with 250g of caster sugar until a light golden brown. Place in the pain d'epices, coating both sides until caramelised. Remove onto greaseproof paper and leave to cool down.

To Serve

Warm the fruits gently, drain the liquor from the fruit, and place around the bowl. Place the pain d'Epices in the centre of the bowl with ice cream on top, and on the ice cream. Add the mulled liquor around.

100
LOWER SLAUGHTER MANOR

Lower Slaughter, Gloucestershire, GL54 2HP

01451 820 456
www.lowerslaughter.co.uk

Lower Slaughter Manor is a luxury country house hotel located in the picturesque village of Lower Slaughter, right in the heart of the Cotswolds. Privately owned by Andrew and Christina Brownsword, this stunning 17th Century manor house combines opulent interiors with traditional charm, attentive service and a relaxed ambience.

Lower Slaughter is considered to be among the prettiest villages in England and is a popular destination all year round for guests wishing to escape to the countryside. The area is perfect for discovering the Cotswolds on foot or venturing further afield to the thriving market towns of Stow-on-the-Wold, Moreton-in-Marsh and Chipping Campden.

Of course with such elegant surroundings to enjoy, guests may not wish to leave the hotel; preferring instead to relax in the drawing rooms, find a quiet corner in the gardens, engage in some energetic tennis or just relax.

Time spent in one of the prettiest villages in England can only ever be a pleasure and at Lower Slaughter Manor, staff ensure that visitors enjoy the stunning surrounds.

The Sixteen58 Restaurant is a stylish venue for fine dining in the Cotswolds, decorated in a contemporary style, giving the dining room a relaxed ambiance. Part of the original chapel retains the large open stone fireplace and forms an anteroom to the main dining area, perfect for a small party of up to 14 guests.

Sixteen58 is also renowned for its award-winning cuisine. Talented chefs always use the finest local, seasonal produce creating menus that are accomplished in execution and full of flavour.

The hotel accommodates smaller parties in a private dining room, the Panel Room, which dates back to the 17th Century and has a sculptured ceiling, splendid panelling and an original, handsome, pillared fireplace.

Lower Slaughter Manor owners Andrew and Christina Brownsword are renowned for high standards.
The couple also own Gidleigh Park, The Bath Priory, Sydney House Chelsea, The Arthouse and ABode Hotels. They added Amberley Castle, Buckland Manor, Lower Slaughter Manor and The Slaughters Country Inn to their portfolio in October 2011. Mr Brownsword said, "I am very proud to be custodian of these hotels." He added that great work had gone into elevating standards of comfort and hospitality under the Brownsword Hotels umbrella.

CRAB RAVIOLI, STIR-FRY SHITAKE & MANGETOUT, LEMONGRASS SAUCE

SERVES 4

 Albarino, Abadia de San Campo Rias Baixas 2011 (Spain)

Ingredients

Saffron Ravioli

250g '00' pasta flour (sifted)
4g salt
3 egg yolks
1 whole egg
10 - 20ml water
nice pinch of saffron powder
15ml olive oil

Crab Ravioli Mousse

75g scallop meat
50ml cream
10ml shellfish *reduction*
1 egg yolk
250g prime white crabmeat
lemon juice
cayenne (tiny pinch)
1/2 tbsp coriander (chopped)
salt and pepper (to taste)

Orange Oil

40g orange peel (chopped)
200ml olive oil

Lemongrass Sauce

100g shallots (sliced)
250g button mushrooms (sliced)
75g unsalted butter
1 turbot carcass (if fish stock is weak)
500ml Gewurztraminer wine
500ml fish stock
500ml cream
140g lemongrass
salt and pepper
sprig lemon thyme

Vegetables

100g mangetout
100g shitake mushrooms
100g bok-choi
sesame seeds (sprinkling of)
1 tbsp oil

Method

For The Ravioli

In a saucepan, place the water, olive oil and saffron. Heat until steaming hot, then leave to cool a little. Pass half the saffron mixture onto the eggs, making sure that you scrape all the saffron in. Sift the flour and salt and place in a blender. Add remaining half to the liquid and blend for five to eight seconds. Scrape down the sides and check the consistency by bringing some of the mix together in your hand. Add more liquid if required - there is a fine line between pasta being too wet and too dry. Bring mix together and allow to rest for at least one hour, then roll out. To make the ravioli, cut circles into the pasta, one should be slightly larger than the other. Brush the inside rim of both with beaten egg yolk.

For The Mousse

Place scallop meat, cream, yolk and shellfish *reduction* into a blender and blend until smooth. Spatula into a bowl over ice. Season. Fold in the crabmeat carefully. Season with cayenne, lemon juice, coriander, salt and pepper. Allow mousse to rest for 20 minutes. Cook off a small tester and check seasoning. Put in a piping bag and pipe mousse filling inside one circle of pasta. Place the other on top and gently press down, so as to remove air without piercing the pasta. Set aside.

For The Orange Oil

Heat the oil with the chopped orange peel until 80°C, then place into a blender and leave to blend for five minutes. Pass through a muslin cloth and leave to cool.

For The Lemongrass Sauce

In a saucepan, sweat the shallots and lemongrass in 50g butter with a pinch of salt (no colour). Add the mushrooms and lemon thyme and sweat until mushrooms are slippery in look (add the turbot carcass and sweat for a further five minutes - you do not need to use the turbot carcass if the fish stock has a strong flavour). Add the fish stock and reduce by half. Separately reduce the wine by a third and add to the reduced stock. Now add the cream, bring to a boil and reduce to required consistency. Pass through *chinois* and whisk in the remaining 25g butter. Check seasoning.

For The Vegetables

Stir-fry very fine *julienne* mangetout, shitake, bok-choi, sesame seeds and oil. Use the lemongrass sauce to bind.

To Serve

Drop the ravioli into boiling water for five minutes. Remove, drain and place two on each plate and assemble as in photograph.

CREEDY CARVER DUCK, TURNIP & GINGER PUREE, CHINESE PANCAKE, ORANGE & ANISE SAUCE

SERVES 4

 Torrontes Selection Terrazas do los Andes 2010
Mendoza (Argentina)

Ingredients

4 duck breasts (with skin)

Pancakes
60ml buttermilk
60ml milk
75g self-raising flour
25g butter (melted)
2 medium eggs

Turnip And Ginger Purée
100g turnips (peeled and thinly sliced)
20g fresh ginger (peeled and thinly sliced)
25g butter
1 orange (zest of)
vegetable stock (enough to cover)
50ml cream

Anise Sauce
500ml chicken stock
1 garlic clove (crushed)
1 orange (zest of)
1 lemon (zest of)
2 sprigs thyme
1 tsp five spice
1 star anise
5 peppercorns

Vegetables
100g baby turnips (whole)
3 spring onions (finely sliced)
olive oil
knob of butter
$1/2$ tsp five spice
100g bok-choi, cut into thick strips
sesame oil
sesame seeds (to garnish)

Method

For The Pancakes
Combine all of the pancake ingredients in a large bowl, whisk until smooth and set aside.

For The Duck
Score the duck breast and season to taste with salt and pepper. Panfry, without any oil, on a high heat, skin side down for four to five minutes until the skin is golden and crisp. Cook on the other side for a further five to six minutes for pink. Remove the duck from the pan, cover with foil and set aside to rest in a warm place. Retain the pan with the duck juices.

> **Chef's Tip**
> Duck is best served pink, though if you want to cook it right through, just leave in the pan for a further two or three minutes. However, leave it too long and it will become tough.

For The Purée
To make the purée, gently sweat the sliced turnips and ginger in the butter until translucent. Add the orange zest and enough stock and cream to cover. Once the turnips are cooked, blend until smooth. Keep warm.

For The Anise Sauce
Deglaze the duck pan and add garlic, orange and lemon zest, thyme and spices. Bring to a boil, reduce to a simmer and cook for ten to 15 minutes. Skim off the residual fat, strain through a fine sieve and return to the pan to reduce to a thick glaze.

To Serve
Simmer the baby turnips in boiling water until tender. Drain and keep warm.

Heat another pan and melt a knob of butter. Cook two thin pancakes until golden and set aside until cool enough to handle.

Sauté the spring onions in a little olive oil with the five spice. Take a pancake and place a spoonful of onions into the middle of each, then fold into the centre. Place in the middle of the serving plate.

Just before serving, wilt the bok-choi in a little sesame oil. Thickly slice the rested duck breast and serve with the remaining ingredients.

DARK CHOCOLATE TART

SERVES 8

 Fonseca 10 Year Old Tawny Port (Portugal)

Ingredients

8 x 10cm rings or moulds

Filling
200g dark chocolate
200ml double cream
80ml milk
1 egg

Sweet Pastry
500g plain flour
3 eggs
300g butter
75g caster
75g icing sugar

Chocolate Sticks
120ml sugar syrup (1:1 sugar syrup)
20g glucose
60g cocoa powder

Confit Orange
15 oranges
sugar syrup (enough to cover - this will depend on the size of your pan)

Orange Sorbet
200g *confited* orange (see method)
400ml orange juice
150ml orange stock (syrup from *confit*)
1 lemon (juice of)

Hazelnut Crumble
375g milk powder
150g hazelnuts (whole)
40g cornflour
225g caster sugar
240g butter
15g salt

Method

For The Filling
Melt chocolate over a *bain-marie*. Bring cream and milk to a boil. Pour onto the whisked whole egg and blend. Slowly add the cream and milk to the melted chocolate using a spatula in small amounts. Pour into the moulds and set.

For The Sweet Pastry
Cream the butter and sugar in a processor. Sift in the flour. After reaching the breadcrumb stage, add beaten eggs and beat until it just comes together. Turn out onto a surface and clingfilm. Put in fridge for a couple of hours to rest. Roll into sheets and freeze. Cook at 160°C for eight to 12 minutes. Punch out into 10cm diameter circles.

Return to oven for two to three minutes. Store in airtight container. When ready to serve top with the set chocolate.

> **Chef's Tip**
>
> For a presentational flourish, try using different shaped cake rings, such as oval, arch, hexagon or star-shaped.

For The Chocolate Sticks
Place all ingredients in saucepan. Heat until it becomes sticky. Put into a piping bag. Leave to set for five minutes. Pipe small lines onto a baking sheet. Cook at 170°C for six minutes.

For The Confit Orange
Score the oranges, taking care not to cut into the centre. *Blanch* and refresh ten times. *Confit* – poach slowly - in sugar syrup for three to four hours on very low heat covered with a lid.

For The Orange Sorbet
Place the orange, orange juice and orange stock syrup in a blender. Blend to a fine coulis and adjust the texture and taste with the juice of one lemon. Pass through a fine sieve and freeze.

For The Hazelnut Crumble
Put everything onto a baking tray at 160°C for seven minute intervals, breaking down each time. Repeat three to four times.

To Serve
Assemble as in photograph.

Lower Slaughter wine matchings by Philippe Boucheron. www.pboucheron.com

110
THE NUT TREE INN

Main Street, Murcott, Oxon OX5 2RE

01865 331 253
www.nuttreeinn.co.uk

t's a family affair at The Nut Tree Inn. After being brought up on his Oxfordshire family farm, chef Mike North bought his local pub and is now ably supported by his fiancée Imogen, juggling front of house while managing his young family of three children, and his sister supports as sous in the kitchen. Following experience with some of the UK's finest chefs, including Marco Pierre White, Michael Caines and Raymond Blanc at Le Manoir, he now applies his classic training into creating equally classic British pub food, but with his own Michelin style.

Mike has a smallholding at the rear of this picturesque Grade II listed country pub. He keeps pigs and sources much of his produce from farming friends, family and local suppliers, who often drop by with a side of venison, brace of pheasants, rabbits and foraged produce.

Mike communicates the seasons perfectly on every dish, contributing to his Which? Good Food Guide five points and winner of Best Use of Local Produce award 2010. He has also held a Michelin star for the past five years.

Customers travel from far and wide to sample The Nut Tree's acclaimed wine list, which offers a diverse range of bins, to relax in the rear courtyard in the Summer, or to shelter inside by the open fires in the Winter.

Relish the region's exclusive offers.
See page 003 for details.

A close team work in the kitchens at The Nut Tree - close due to family ties, but also due to the small size of the kitchen. Mike is over 6ft and the rest of the brigade dance like a troop of ballerinas on a busy service, creating beautifully balanced dishes, with perfect depth of flavour focusing on Great British classics. Mike's pork belly has remained on the menu since they began in 2006 due to customer demand.

PAVE OF HOME SMOKED SALMON WITH WHIPPED HORSERADISH CREAM, AVRUGA CAVIAR

SERVES 10

 Morgon 2011 - From Domaine Marcel Lapierre (France)

Ingredients

To Cure The Salmon

1 side salmon (skin scored)
1kg Maldon sea salt
1kg fine table salt
1kg caster sugar
1 lemon (zest and juice of)
1 orange (zest and juice of)
100ml brandy

Horseradish Cream

250ml double cream
200g fresh horseradish root
50ml white wine vinegar
icing sugar (to taste)

To Smoke The Salmon

1kg fine oak sawdust

Garnish

1 Avruga caviar
salad leaves
lemon juice
olive oil

Method

To Cure The Salmon (Prepare the day before)

Mix all the ingredients together and rub the salmon with the salt mix then place the salmon in a plastic container. Cover completely with the remaining mixture and weigh down. Cover with clingfilm and leave for 24 hours. When ready, remove the salmon from the container. Wash off excess salt mixture and pat dry.

> **Chef's Tip**
> If affordable and when in season try to use wild salmon.

For The Horseradish Cream (Prepare at least six hours before serving)

Finely grate the horseradish root and mix with the vinegar. Add icing sugar to taste. Add the mixture to the cream and leave to infuse for six hours. When ready, pass the cream through a fine sieve to remove the horseradish. Whisk until soft peaks form and chill. Reserve until ready.

To Smoke The Salmon (Prepare at least six hours before serving)

Heat the sawdust in a frying pan until it sets on fire. Place the sawdust into a large heatproof pan and cover immediately to extinguish the fire and trap in the smoke. Place the salmon onto a cooling rack and place over the smoking pan. Wrap the entire pan and salmon in a bin liner to trap in the smoke and flavour the salmon. Leave to infuse for six hours in the fridge. When ready, unwrap and discard the sawdust. Remove the skin from the salmon and trim all the fat. Pave cut the salmon into ten pieces (split the side of salmon down the middle lengthways, remove the skin and cut into portions).

To Serve

Plate up one 'pavé' with a rocher of the chilled horseradish cream and garnish with Avruga caviar and salad leaves dressed with lemon juice and olive oil.

SLOW ROAST BELLY OF PORK WITH CELERIAC PUREE, SALT & VINEGAR POTATOES & APPLE GRAVY

SERVES 6 - 8

Spätburgunder, Blauschiefer, 2011 - Meyer-Näkel, AHR (Germany)

Ingredients

Pork Belly

1 boned pork belly (split length ways and tied)
1 onion (chopped)
2 sticks celery (chopped)
fine picked herbs

Apple Gravy

500ml veal stock
2 Bramley apples chopped
100ml Calvados
200ml dry cider
500ml cooking liquor (from the belly pork)
50g butter

Celeriac Purée

1 celeriac (peeled and diced)
milk and cream (to cover)
salt and pepper

Salt And Vinegar Potatoes

50g unsalted butter
8 waxy potatoes
white wine vinegar
water
salt

Garnish

seasonal vegetables (to accompany)
pea shoots

Method

For The Pork Belly

Place the pork belly into a large, deep roasting tray and cover with water. Season to taste with salt and pepper and add the chopped vegetables. Cover with foil and braise at 150°C for six hours. Leave to cool in the stock. Remove the pork from the stock (reserving the cooking liquor) and roast in a preheated 200°C oven for 20 to 25 minutes, or until the skin has gone a lovely golden brown and has produced good, crispy crackling.

> **Chef's Tip**
>
> Always use free range pork and don't be afraid of the fat as this is where the flavour comes from and will render out during the cooking process.

For The Apple Gravy

Caramelise the apple in the butter then add the Calvados and reduce to a syrup. Add the cider and reduce by half. Add the veal stock and cooking liquor and reduce by approximately half to a light sauce consistency. Season with salt and pepper to taste and pass through a fine sieve.

For The Celeriac Purée

Place the diced celeriac in a dish and cover with the milk and cream. Simmer gently for about 15 minutes or until the celeriac is completely tender. Remove the celeriac from the milk and cream mixture. Place celeriac in a liquidiser and blend until smooth, adding the milk and cream mixture as required to produce a silky smooth purée that just holds its shape. Season with salt and pepper to taste and pass through a fine sieve.

For The Salt And Vinegar Potatoes

Peel and chop the potatoes into 1cm cubes. Place in a pan and cover with equal parts water and white wine vinegar. Season heavily with salt and gently simmer until potatoes are tender. Remove from the heat and reserve in the liquid until needed.

When ready to serve, fry the potato cubes in butter in a sauté pan until golden brown.

To Serve

Place a spoonful of the celeriac purée in a bowl and spread. Cut a good thick slice of the crispy pork belly and place on top. Arrange the salt and vinegar potatoes around the pork and pour over the apple gravy. Garnish with the pea shoots and serve.

STICKY TOFFEE PUDDING WITH CARAMELISED APPLE TART, PRALINE CREAM & PRALINE ICE CREAM

SERVES 8

 Oloroso Abocado - Alameda - Hidalgo (Spain)

Ingredients

Sticky Toffee Pudding

125g dates
150ml water
75g butter
190g soft brown sugar
3 eggs
225g self raising flour
2 tsp bicarbonate of soda

Caramelised Apple Tart

1 sheet ready roll puff pastry
4 Bramley apples
50g butter
100g sugar

Praline Cream

420ml milk
3 egg yolks
20g sugar
1g cornflour
praline paste (to taste)

Toffee Sauce

100g soft brown sugar
100g butter
100ml double cream

Praline Ice Cream

850ml milk, 850ml cream
120g sugar
6 egg yolks
praline paste (to taste)

Garnish

fresh mint

Chef's Tip

Try to use Medjool dates as this is where the toffee flavour comes from. The better the dates the better the flavour.

Method

For The Sticky Toffee Pudding

Add water and the dates into a pan and bring to a boil. Transfer to a food processor and blitz with the butter.

Mix together the bicarbonate of soda and the flour and pass through a fine sieve. Whisk together the eggs and the date mixture and add the flour in three stages. Place in a baking tray and put in a 180°C preheated oven for approximately 45 minutes or until cooked.

For The Caramelised Apple Tart

Cut the puff pastry into round discs, about the size of the apple. Place between two trays and bake for ten minutes.

Peel four apples and cut in half with a round cutter so they are the same size as the pastry discs.

Meanwhile, in a pan, heat the butter with the sugar to make a caramel. Caramelise the apples on both sides until soft then remove from the pan to cool. Place the apple onto the pastry and put aside until needed.

For The Praline Cream

Whisk the milk together and desired amount of praline paste to taste and bring to a boil. Cream together the egg yolks, sugar, flour and cornflour, then add the mixture into the pan and bring back to a boil until the sauce thickens. Place the mixture into a plastic container and cover the surface with clingfilm.

For The Toffee Sauce

Melt the butter and sugar. Add the cream and bring to a boil. Remove and stir to stop skin forming.

For The Praline Ice Cream

Put the milk and cream into a pan with half of the sugar and the praline paste to taste. Bring to a boil. Cream together the other half of the sugar and the egg yolks and pour over the boiling cream. Whisk until smooth and leave to cool. Churn in an ice cream machine, or freeze for two to three hours, stirring every ten to 15 minutes, to break up any ice crystals.

To Serve

Cut the sticky toffee pudding into fingers 2.5cm x 12.5cm, place in a pan and cover with the toffee sauce. Bring to a simmer. Meanwhile, place the apple tart into the oven to warm through. Arrange as in picture. Garnish with mint.

120
RONNIE'S OF THORNBURY

11 St Mary Street, Thornbury, South Gloucestershire, BS35 2AB

01454 411 137
www.ronnies-restaurant.co.uk

Chef patron Ron Faulkner has an impressive food pedigree. His distinguished career has seen him work in some of the most prestigious kitchens in the UK and Europe, for celebrated chefs such as Anton Mosimann and Ed Baines. Schooled in classic French techniques, Ron's modern European cooking style is underpinned with a passion for using the very best seasonal ingredients.

Ronnie's of Thornbury is a popular venue for those travelling en route to the South West and the Cotswolds. A restaurant with a coffee lounge serving brunch, lunch and dinner is housed within a sympathetically renovated, 17th Century building with beamed ceilings and natural stonework walls. It is the perfect setting for a menu that is an eclectic mix, based on personal taste and sound cooking techniques, rather than any particular country's cuisine.

An underlying feature is a core of excellent ingredients, local where possible and carefully chosen. Ronnie's is a Which? readers award-winner and passionate promoter of regional producers.

South African born chef Ron, brings his passions for local fayre, quality of ingredients and art to his much loved neighbourhood restaurant. The walls are adorned with artwork by some of the UK's leading artists and his kitchens stocked by some of the leading suppliers from the Cotswolds, the South West and Wales.

HOT & COLD SMOKED MERE FARM RAINBOW TROUT

SERVES 6

 Macon-Solutre, Clos des Bertillonnes, Domaine Robert-Denogent 2009 (France)

Ingredients

2 hot smoked rainbow trout fillets
200g cold smoked rainbow trout (sliced)

Cheese Filling

200g cream cheese
1 tbsp milk
1 lemon
2 tbsp snipped chives

Buckwheat Crêpes

60g plain flour
60g buckwheat flour
2 large eggs
225ml whole milk
1 tsp table salt

Potato Salad

200g new potatoes
1 tsp cumin seeds
2 tbsp mayonnaise
4 tbsp crème fraîche
3 tbsp snipped chives
1 tbsp horseradish (freshly grated)
salt and pepper (freshly ground)
trimmings from the hot smoked trout

Garnish

6 quail's eggs (soft boiled)
1 pickled banana shallot
1 tbsp capers
2 sprigs parsley (deep fried)

Method

For The Buckwheat Crêpes

Make the buckwheat crêpe batter by sifting all the dry ingredients into a mixing bowl, make a well in the centre and crack the eggs into the well. Whisk the eggs, slowly incorporating the flour. Add the milk slowly to loosen the mixture and leave it to rest for half an hour. Using a non-stick pan, cook the crêpes, making sure you have four crêpes, no thicker than 2mm. Leave to cool.

For The Cheese Filling

Make the cheese filling by simply beating all the ingredients together and season well with freshly milled salt and pepper.

For The Cold Smoked Trout Mille-Feuille

Place the crêpes on top of each other and cut into a rectangle, approximately 8cm by 18cm. Cover each crêpe with a thin spreading of the cream cheese mixture. Place an even layer of the cold smoked trout over each crêpe. Stack the crêpes with cheese filling on top of the trout. Top the stack with a layer of trout.

For The Hot Smoked Trout And Potato Salad

Separate the hot smoked fillets by cutting down the centre line. Cut the thick fillets into six diamonds per fillet. Keep the thin fillets and trimmings for the salad. Boil the new potatoes in salted water with the cumin seeds and leave to cool. Remove the skins and cut into cubes. Bind the potatoes with the trout trimmings, remaining ingredients and season.

To Serve

Cut the cold smoked trout mille-feuille into six rectangles and place at one end of the plate. Directly opposite, place a neat pile of potato salad and top with two trout diamonds on each. Garnish the centre of the plate with the soft boiled quail's eggs, capers, pickled shallots and parsley.

Chef's Tip

Smoked salmon is a poor substitute for the trout, which has a beautiful delicate flavour and texture. The cream cheese has twice as many layers as the trout or buckwheat crêpe, so use sparingly.

LAMB WITH SPRING VEGETABLES & ROSEMARY POTATO

SERVES 6

🍷 *Château Vieux Robin Bois de Lunier 2007*
(France)

Ingredients

Lamb
6 x 150g spring lamb loin steaks (no fat)
200ml red wine *jus*
3 spring lamb's kidneys
1 egg (lightly beaten)
100g seasoned flour
100g Panko breadcrumbs
1 tbsp parsley (chopped)
salt and pepper (freshly milled)

Carrot Purée
2 large carrots
200g unsalted butter

Spring Vegetables
120g peas (freshly shelled)
120g broad beans (freshly podded)
12 baby carrots
12 spears asparagus

Rosemary Potatoes
3 large Maris Piper potatoes
2 sprigs rosemary
250g unsalted butter
2 cloves garlic

Method

For The Rosemary Potatoes

Cut the bottom and top edge off the potatoes to form cylinders with a flat top and bottom. Cut four, 1.5cm thick, discs out of each cylinder. Shape each disc into a barrel shape with a sharp knife. Cook the potatoes by placing them in a heavy-bottomed pan with the butter, garlic and rosemary over a low flame. Once golden brown, turn and cook the other side. They are cooked when a knife passes through with no resistance.

For The Spring Vegetables

Peel the carrots and asparagus. *Blanch* and refresh all the vegetables separately so they are just cooked. Peel the skins from the broad beans.

For The Carrot Purée

Peel and boil the carrots in salted water until tender and drain. Liquidise the carrots with butter and season. Set aside the purée and keep warm until needed.

For The Lamb Kidneys

Cut the kidneys in half and remove the central sinews. Coat the kidneys in flour, dip in the beaten egg and coat with the Panko crumbs. Panfry the kidneys over a moderate heat with butter for approximately three minutes on each side. Once golden brown, remove from the heat, dust with chopped parsley and leave to rest.

For The Lamb Loin

Season the loin with freshly milled salt and pepper. Cook the meat by sealing it in a hot pan. Once it is coloured nicely, add a knob of butter to the pan and finish in a moderate oven for five to eight minutes. Remove the meat from the oven and leave to rest.

> **Chef's Tip**
>
> The best way to check if your meat is cooked is to probe it with a thermometer. A temperature of 45°C, left to rest for ten minutes, will cook the meat medium rare. Note the final temperature after resting will be about 56°C.

To Serve

Warm the purée and red wine *jus*. Reheat the potatoes, lamb loins and kidneys in the oven for two to three minutes. To reheat the vegetables, plunge into boiling water for a minute, drain and place in a pan with a knob of butter and season.

Cut the lamb loin in half, place a spoonful of purée on each plate and arrange the vegetables and lamb evenly on the plates. Spoon some of the *jus* over and serve.

PASSION FRUIT PANNA COTTA, ROASTED PINEAPPLE & MANGO SORBET

SERVES 6

*Botrytised Viognier 2010, Trinity Hill
(New Zealand)*

Ingredients

Panna Cotta Base

1.5 ltr whole milk
80g caster sugar
3 leaves bronze gelatine
1 x (8cm x 18cm) mould

Passion Fruit Topping

150ml passion fruit purée
50ml water
60g caster sugar
2 leaves bronze gelatine
2 passion fruit

Mango Sorbet

60g caster sugar
100ml water
120ml mango purée
1 egg white

Mango Gel

180ml mango purée
40g caster sugar
$1^1/_2$g agar agar

Roasted Pineapple

1 large pineapple
freshly cracked pepper

Garnish

6 coconut tuiles

Method

For The Panna Cotta

Bring the milk to a boil, reduce to 500ml, add the sugar and liquidise to re-incorporate the milk solids. Soak the gelatine in cold water and add to the hot condensed milk, mixing thoroughly. Line a mould (approximately 8cm x 18cm) with a sheet of clingfilm. Pour the condensed milk into the mould and place in a fridge to cool and set for two to three hours.

For The Passion Fruit Topping

Bring all the ingredients to a boil, scooping in the fruit from the passion fruit. Soak the gelatine in cold water and add to the hot liquid. Leave to cool. Once the passion fruit liquid is at room temperature, pour it onto the panna cotta which should be set.

> **Chef's Tip**
>
> Place an upside down ramekin in the pot with the milk while you reduce it. This will stop the milk from boiling over. The milk should be reduced as quickly as possible without letting it stick to the bottom of the pan.

For The Mango Sorbet

Place the sugar and water in a pan and heat until the sugar is dissolved. Add the mango purée and pour into an ice cream churner. Add the egg white and churn until set. Transfer to a container and freeze.

For The Mango Gel

Place all the ingredients into a pan and bring to a boil. Simmer for three minutes and leave to cool. Once set, liquidise.

For The Roasted Pineapple

Cut the pineapple six slices, about 1.5cm thick. Using a cutter, cut the slice into a disc, removing the skin and cut out the core. Season with freshly cracked pepper and grill in a non-stick pan.

To Serve

Take the edges off the panna cotta with a sharp, hot knife and cut into six nice slices. Place a spoonful of the gel on each plate, drag a spoon through it and place the panna cotta on top. Place a piece of roasted pineapple on each plate and top with mango sorbet. Garnish with a coconut tuile and serve.

130
THE STAR INN

Watery Lane, Sparsholt, Wantage, Oxfordshire, OX12 9PL

01235 751 873
www.thestarsparsholt.co.uk

For over 300 years, The Star Inn has been at the heart of the village of Sparsholt - an idyllic village nestling at the foot of the ancient Ridgeway path with its world famous White Horse and its miles of unspoilt trails.

At the heart of The Star is the traditional and relaxed pub bar with great real ales, quality lagers and a carefully selected wine list. Add to this an open, bright, rustic country pub feel with flagstone floors and wide windows looking out to the garden. The ethos is relaxed, comfortable, warm and inviting with great attention to detail in the food created by chef Dave Watts, highlighted as 'Chef to Watch in 2013' by The Good Food Guide. The menus reflect the seasons with Summer dishes to be enjoyed in the garden and hearty Winter fayre by the fire, no pretence, just a warm welcome for you (and your dog!)

Chef Dave's food ethos is about the care he takes over sourcing produce, with much of it coming from the local area, supporting the local community. It must be ethical, sustainable and responsibly produced.

Accommodation housed in a converted barn a stone's throw away from the main pub. Newly refurbished combining contemporary with rustic style, the emphasis is on comfort with each room furnished with the highest quality beds to ensure an excellent night's sleep.

Relish the region's exclusive offers.
See page 003 for details.

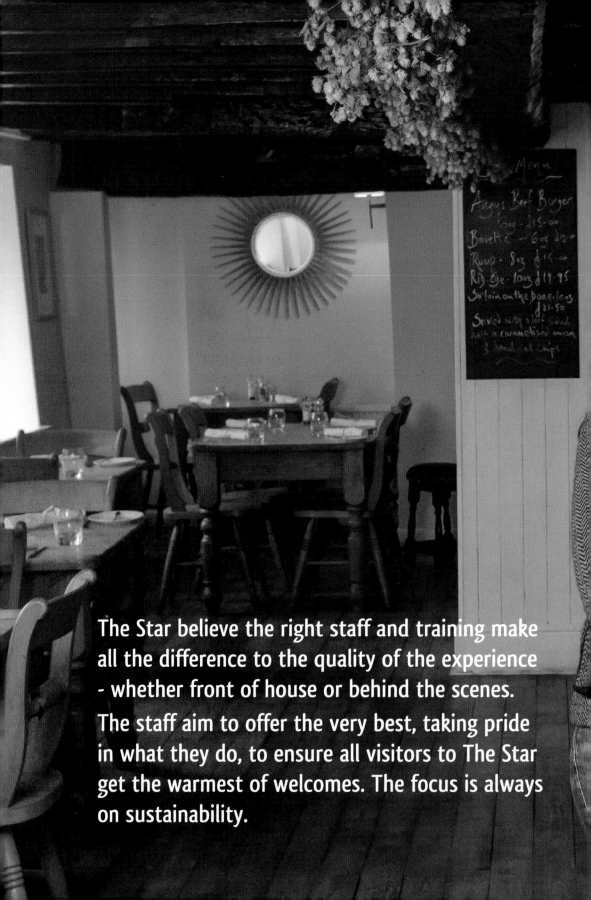

The Star believe the right staff and training make all the difference to the quality of the experience - whether front of house or behind the scenes.

The staff aim to offer the very best, taking pride in what they do, to ensure all visitors to The Star get the warmest of welcomes. The focus is always on sustainability.

Bar Snacks

Scotch Egg &
Wholegrain Mayonnaise
£2.50

Honey Roasted
Cashews
£3.00

Crispy Whitebait
Marie-Rose
£2.50

Hand Cut Chips
£3.00

BEETROOT, GOAT'S CHEESE & MUSTARD

SERVES 4

 Loimer Grüner Veltliner 2010
(Austria)

Ingredients

Roasted Beetroots

3 ruby beetroots
3 candy beetroots (reserve one for the carpaccio)
3 golden beetroots
1 bottle cider vinegar
salt and black pepper
Cotswold Gold rapeseed oil

Goat's Cheese And Mustard Purée

125g potato (peeled and thinly sliced)
50g strong hard goat's cheese (Rachel washed
rind hard goat's cheese. Reserve some to serve)
pinch of salt
35ml Cotswold Gold rapeseed oil
twist of black pepper
1 tsp English mustard

Beetroot And Sourdough Crumb

1 beetroot (roughly the size of a tennis ball)
1g caraway seeds
8g yellow mustard seeds
2g coarse sea salt
twist of black pepper
30g sourdough (toasted and blended
to a fine crumb)
15ml Cotswold Gold rapeseed oil

Mustard Dressing

35g Dijon mustard
25ml white wine vinegar
2 pinch salt
50ml water
200ml Cotswold Gold rapeseed oil

Candy Beetroot Carpaccio

1 candy beetroot (reserved from roasted beetroots)
pinch salt
mustard dressing

Garnish

small bag rocket or mixed baby leaves

Method

Roasted Beetroots

Place each colour beetroot into the centre of a sheet of tinfoil
and season. Wrap into a parcel and place onto a baking tray.
Put into a preheated oven at 180°C and cook for 45 to 60
minutes. Remove from the oven and allow to cool enough so
you can handle them. Peel the skins off. Keep the ruby beetroot
in a separate bowl to the other two colours. Reserve one candy
beetroot for the carpaccio. Cut the remaining beetroots into
sixes and season with a pinch of salt, black pepper, a glug of
rapeseed oil and a dash of cider vinegar.

> **Chef's Tip**
>
> Try and get a variety of colours. I use ruby, candy
> and golden. You could also use white if you can find it.
> Wash well.

Goat's Cheese And Mustard Purée

Cook potatoes slowly for one hour in 500ml water at
approximately 65°C. Once cooked, remove from the water (retain
100ml) and place in a blender. Add the 100ml of cooking liquid
and the rest of the ingredients, blend until smooth.

Beetroot And Sourdough Crumb

Peel and finely slice the beetroot and dry in the oven at 80°C for
two hours. Toast the seeds for two minutes at 180°C. Place all of
the ingredients into a blender and blend to a powder. Add all of
the other ingredients and combine.

Mustard Dressing

Place the mustard, vinegar, salt and water into a bowl, whisk slowly
adding the oil into the other ingredients to create a dressing.

Candy Beetroot Carpaccio

Finely slice with a sharp knife or use a Japanese mandolin, then
season with a pinch of salt and mustard dressing.

To Serve

Take the purée and spread it onto the plate. Arrange the
beetroots and crumble chunks of the reserved goat's cheese
around, then sprinkle with the crumb. Position the beetroot
carpaccio and add a handful of baby leaves. Dress with a little
more mustard dressing.

ROASTED YORKSHIRE GROUSE, CELERIAC, QUINOA & BLACKBERRIES

SERVES 4

🍷 *2008 Chateau Lyonnat, Saint-Emilion (France)*

Ingredients

4 oven-ready grouse taken to the crown
(ask your butcher to keep you all of the bones)
1 pack (100g) baby spinach

Roasted Celeriac Purée

250g celeriac (peeled and diced)
15ml rapeseed oil
75g butter, 2 pinches salt
375ml semi-skimmed milk
1 dsp lemon juice

Quinoa

100g quinoa
300ml white chicken stock
pinch of salt
5g linseeds, 10g poppy seeds
50ml rapeseed oil

Macerated Blackberries

60g blackberries (12 x large)
pinch salt
1 tsp sugar
grind of black pepper
60ml Crème de Mure (a blackberry liqueur)
(boiled)
1 tsp red wine vinegar

Grouse Sauce

bones from the 4 grouse (chopped)
1 tbsp vegetable oil, 30g butter
500ml brown chicken stock (reduced by half)
250ml red wine (reduced by half)
50g blackberries
30ml double cream
60ml Crème de Mure (boiled)
5 juniper berries (crushed)
sugar (to season)

Roasting The Grouse

1 clove garlic, 1 sprig thyme
2 tbsp vegetable oil
4 grouse crowns
salt and black pepper

Method

For The Roasted Celeriac Purée

Roast the celeriac in the oil until it starts to colour. Add the butter, little by little, until the celeriac is golden brown, strain and reserve the butter. Place the celeriac salt and milk into a pan and bring to a boil, simmer for five minutes then strain, reserving the milk. Place the celeriac, butter, lemon juice and 150ml of the milk, blend until smooth.

For The Roasted Quinoa

Roast the quinoa for 15 minutes at 180°C. Place into a saucepan, add the chicken stock and salt and cook for 20 minutes. Once cooked, remove from the heat and leave to cool (keeping covered). Toast the seeds for two minutes at 180°C. Combine all of the ingredients and keep warm.

For The Macerated Blackberries

Combine all of the ingredients, keep warm (around 25°C).

For The Grouse Sauce

Heat the oil in a large frying pan and add the chopped bones, colouring slightly then add the butter. Continue to cook until golden brown. Strain the bones and *deglaze* the pan with a tablespoon of water. Add this to the brown chicken stock.

Place all of the ingredients into a saucepan except the blackberries. Bring to a boil and skim. Turn to a medium heat and cook for 30 minutes. Add the blackberries and return to the boil for a minute. Strain through a sieve into a clean saucepan. Place onto a high heat and reduce to a coating consistency. Season with salt, sugar and fresh ground black pepper.

Roasting The Grouse

Preheat the oven to 160°C. Season each grouse with a pinch of salt and place them into the pan, skinside down, with a little vegetable oil. Turn the birds colouring evenly on all sides. Once coloured remove from the pan, add the garlic and thyme, allow to flavour the oil in the pan. Pour this onto an oventray and place the grouse on top of this. Cook for eight minutes. Remove from the oven once cooked and leave in a warm place to rest for four minutes.

To Serve

Wilt four handfuls of baby spinach in a pan of butter and season to taste. Place the warmed purée onto warm plates and scatter over the quinoa. Arrange the spinach and then the blackberries. Bring the sauce to a boil, place the grouse crown onto the plate and spoon over the sauce.

> **Chef's Tip**
>
> Getting your butcher to do all the hard work is a must. I'd also recommend using wild mushrooms if in season.

POACHED PEAR, CELERY & WALNUT

SERVES 4

 *Tokaji Aszú 5
(Hungarian sweet wine)*

Ingredients

Poaching Liquor For The Pears

4 ripe pears
500ml Sauternes (I use Monbazillac)
1 lemon (zest and juice)
250ml water
1 pinch salt

Walnut Ice Cream

250ml whole milk
60g walnut halves
30g caster sugar
2 free range egg yolks
75ml double cream
3 tsp walnut oil

Candied Celery

1 head celery
100g caster sugar
200ml water

Celery Salt

20g celery leaves (only the lighter inner leaves,
not the darker outside ones)
60g celeriac (peeled and *julienned*)
3g course sea salt
10g granulated sugar

Method

For The Poaching Liquor For The Pears

Reduce the wine to 300ml, then add the water, salt, lemon juice
and zest. Bring back to a boil, remove from the heat and leave
for 20 minutes. Peel, halve and core the pears and place them
into a pan. Strain the poaching liquor onto the pears, cover and
cook until the pears are soft but still holding their shape.

Chef's Tip

Leave the pear slightly underdone when you remove
them from the heat - they will absorb more of the liquor
when they rest.

For The Walnut Ice Cream

Bring the milk and walnuts to a boil. Remove from the heat and
leave to infuse for ten minutes, then strain reserving the walnuts.
Whisk together the sugar and the egg yolks. Bring the milk back
to a boil and pour onto the yolks and sugar whilst whisking. In a
blender, combine 30g of the reserved walnuts, the cream and the
walnut oil. Blend until smooth, pass through a sieve and add to
the custard. Put into an ice cream maker and churn.

For The Candied Celery

Remove three sticks from the celery and finely slice. Put into a
pan with the water and bring to a boil, then simmer. Cook for a
further five minutes, then leave to steep for ten minutes.
Take another three sticks of celery, peel and slice thinly on an
angle. Strain off the water into another pan and add the sugar.
Bring to a boil and add the sliced celery, turn down and cook
until transparent.

For The Celery Salt

Dry the celery and celeriac in a low oven around 80°C for
approximately one hour. This needs to be as dry as possible.
Once dry, place into a spice grinder (or pestle and mortar),
add the salt and sugar then grind to a powder.

For The Pear Purée

Take four halves of the poached pears, put into a blender and
purée until smooth.

To Serve

Spoon the purée onto the plates and arrange the candied celery.
Slice each half pear four times from top to bottom, fan out
slightly and place onto each plate. Sprinkle the celery salt over
the plates and add a scoop of the ice cream.

140
THE SWAN INN

Swinbrook, Near Burford, Oxon, OX18 4DY

01993 823 339
www.theswanswinbrook.co.uk

Nestled on the picturesque banks of the River Windrush, The Swan Inn is a million miles from the hustle and bustle of everyday life. From the outside, it appears to be the quintessential English pub. Inside, however, it reveals itself as a boutique Cotswolds Inn with sumptuous rooms, stunning food and breathtaking history.

The Swan Inn provides the perfect base for those seeking a quiet evening drink and for diners seeking fresh, locally sourced food. It is also the ideal location for visitors planning to explore Gloucestershire, Oxfordshire and the Cotswolds.

It's idyllic location, a short distance from the picturesque town of Burford, provides the perfect setting to relax and unwind.

The Swan has a rich history associated with it. The Inn is owned by the Dowager Duchess of Devonshire, the last surviving Mitford sister, and - along with the neighbouring cottage - forms the residual part of the estate inherited by the family at the beginning of the 19th Century. Photographs around the pub celebrate the connections to the Mitfords and village life.

The Inn has been improved by its present owners, Archie and Nicola Orr-Ewing, who were already successfully running The King's Head Inn at Bledington, when they took over in 2006. They are now responsible for both venues and are just as hands-on as the excellent team led by head chef Matt Laughton.

Working closely with the architect appointed by the Dowager Duchess to renovate the impressive Cotswold stone barn, Nicola has stamped her own personality on the styling and interior décor of the accommodation, comprising six beautiful bedrooms and five more due to be completed by the beginning of October 2013. These will overlook the river and will be well worth a visit.

Archie, meanwhile, has taken a close interest in the bar and restaurant, ensuring that every visit is truly memorable. The couple are very much a part of life in the pub and make it their job to see that everyone feels at home.

Echoes of the Mitford Sisters fill the corridors and hallways of the Swan Inn. The stylish aristocrats were headline-makers during the early part of the 20th Century. The eldest Mitford sister, Nancy, became a successful novelist and copies of her books are available for guests. They were inextricably linked to politics, with fellow novelist Jessica and youngest sister Deborah marrying nephews-by-marriage of Prime Ministers Winston Churchill and Harold Macmillan. Large black and white photographs of the Mitfords adorn stairwells, reminding visitors of the former inhabitants. Deborah - or Debo - was responsible for filling the venue with Mitford nostalgia.

FRESH FIG, WATERMELON, OLIVE & FETA SALAD

SERVES 1 (per person)

🍷 *Geoff Merrill South Australian Shiraz-Grenache Rosé 2008*

Method

Whisk the lemon juice, olive oil and balsamic syrup together.

Arrange watermelon and fig wedges on a plate.

Toss leaves in olive oil lemon juice, arrange in centre of plate.

Add diced feta and black olives.

Now drizzle balsamic syrup over salad and sprinkle with pumpkin seeds.

Chef's Tip

Cut the figs into quarters, spoon a little honey over them and a dash of balsamic and a few thyme leaves.
Place under a hot grill to caramelise. This will add a hot element to the salad.

Ingredients

1 fresh fig (cut into quarters)
20g mixed leaves
3 slices watermelon (peeled)
5 black olives
30g Greek feta cheese (diced)
5g pumpkin seeds (toasted)
balsamic syrup
20ml olive oil
$1/4$ lemon (juice)
salt and pepper

CORN-FED CHICKEN BREAST WITH SPICED SWEET POTATOES, ROAST FENNEL & CHORIZO SAUSAGE

SERVES 1 (per person)

St Nicolas de Bourgueil Domaine de la Butte 2006
Jacky Blott (France)

Ingredients

Chicken

1 cornfed chicken breast
salt and pepper
knob of butter
olive oil
sprig fresh thyme

Spiced Sweet Potato

1 sweet potato (peeled and cut into 4)
knob of butter
1 chorizo picante (skin removed and sliced - use
uncooked chorizo)
hot curry powder
ground cumin
smoked paprika

$^{1}/_{4}$ bulb fennel (cut into 3)

Garnish

mixed leaves

Method

For The Fennel

Boil a pan of salted water and cook fennel until just soft.
Refresh in iced water until cold.

For The Chicken

Season the chicken breast with salt and pepper. Heat a small
amount of butter and a little oil in a pan and add the chicken
breast. Brown on both sides, add a sprig of thyme and a
tablespoon of water. Place in oven until cooked - approximately
20 minutes. Allow to rest for at least five minutes before serving.

> **Chef's Tip**
>
> Put the chicken breast into a resealable plastic bag with a
> tablespoon of olive oil, a little lime zest, sprig of thyme and
> a pinch of dry chilli flakes. Seal bag and leave overnight in
> the fridge to add more flavour to the chicken.

For The Spiced Sweet Potatoes

Heat up a little more butter, add sweet potato wedges, spices
and salt. Place in oven at 190°C and turn often to get an even
colouring. When potatoes are nearly cooked, add fennel and
return to oven. Five minutes before serving, add sliced chorizo
and cook for a further five minutes.

To Serve

Arrange sweet potatoes, fennel and chorizo on plate. Arrange a
few mixed leaves on top and finish with the chicken breast.

Dogs on Leads
Bantams
On Loose

TONKA BEAN PANNA COTTA WITH MIXED BERRIES & STRAWBERRY SORBET

SERVES 6

Jurançon Moëlleux Symphonie de Novembre
Domaine Cauhapé (France)

Method

For The Panna Cotta

The day before
Mix cream, milk and Tonka or vanilla together. Cover and leave overnight in fridge.

The next day
Pour the cream mixture into a pan, stir in the sugar and slowly bring to a boil. Drain gelatine and whisk into the mix.

Strain mix through a fine sieve and allow to cool.

Pour into glasses and place in fridge to set for at least two hours.

> **Chef's Tip**
> Heat one glass of red wine with 100g of sugar, a little cinnamon stick and a strip of orange peel. Then, add the berries and poach until just soft. Add juice of half a lime and serve warm with the panna cotta.

Ingredients

750ml double cream
250ml full fat milk
1 Tonka bean or 1 split vanilla pod
(Tonka bean is very hard to get hold of but vanilla is just as good)
350g caster sugar
$2^1/2$ sheets bronze gelatine (soaked in cold water)
strawberry sorbet
seasonal berries

150
THE WHITE HART

Main Road, Fyfield, Abingdon, Oxon, OX13 5LW

01865 390 585
www.whitehart-fyfield.com

I n 2005 current owners, Kay and Mark Chandler, took over this historic 15th Century building, in the picturesque village of Fyfield. Built during the reign of Henry VI as a chantry, The White Hart boasts many original features including a tunnel to Fyfield Manor, which was built at the time of the dissolution of the monasteries. Housing one of the most stunning interiors of any pub in the region, the setting is breathtaking, from the soaring eaves of the great hall and minstrel's gallery, to the bar with a roaring log fire in Winter and terrace full of aromatic herb gardens in Summer.

A firm believer in using local produce, Mark forages in local woodlands and has developed a large kitchen garden where he grows fruit and vegetables for the menu. Kay is the perfect host, offering a warm professional welcome to all her guests. Cooking is modern British with their slow roasted pork belly, with foot long crackling, being a favourite amongst the well-heeled members of the Oxfordshire and Cotswolds society.

The White Hart has held two rosettes for culinary excellence for four years running, yet it is still somewhere you can stop and have a pint of real ale after a hard day's work. It was voted one of the 'Top 50 Gastropubs' in the UK, in a recent industry poll.

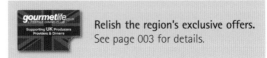

gourmetlife
Supporting UK Producers
Providers & Diners

Relish the region's exclusive offers.
See page 003 for details.

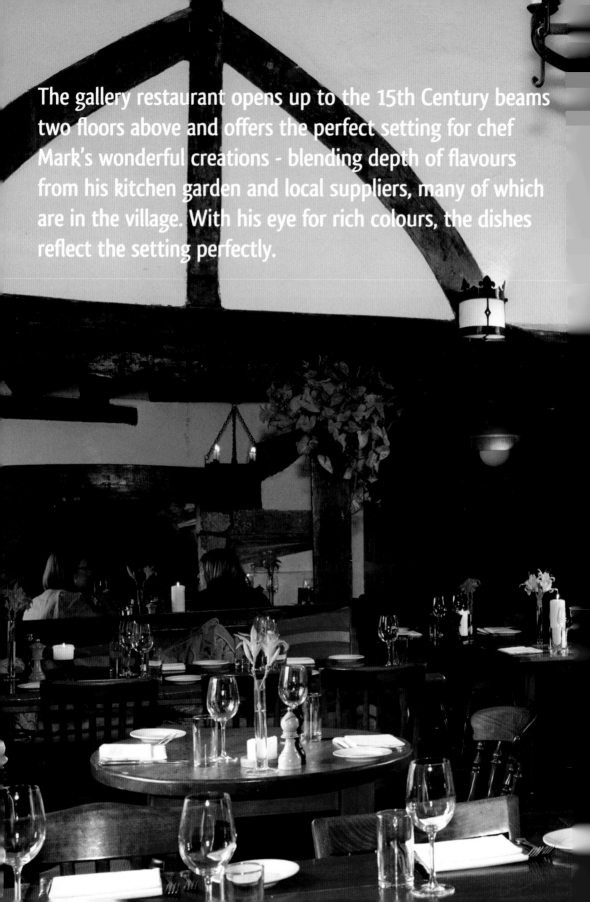

The gallery restaurant opens up to the 15th Century beams two floors above and offers the perfect setting for chef Mark's wonderful creations - blending depth of flavours from his kitchen garden and local suppliers, many of which are in the village. With his eye for rich colours, the dishes reflect the setting perfectly.

SALMON GRAVADLAX, MARINATED CUCUMBER SALAD

SERVES 4

 Vibrant Petit Chablis, Burgundy, 2010 (France)

Ingredients

Gravadlax

500g piece of centre cut salmon fillet (skin on, scaled and pinboned)
50ml vodka
250g rock salt
500g caster sugar
1 tbsp fennel seeds
1 tbsp juniper berries (crushed)
pinch of whole cloves
2 bunches dill (1 roughly chopped and 1 with stalks removed and finely chopped)
French mustard

Cucumber Salad

2 cucumbers (peeled and sliced thinly - we use a mandolin)
table salt
200ml white wine vinegar
200g caster sugar
1 red chilli
1 bay leaf
1 star anise
2 shallots (finely chopped)
$1/2$ bunch chives (chopped)

Dressing

50ml white wine vinegar
1 tbsp French mustard
1 egg yolk
1 tsp caster sugar
$1/2$ tsp salt
freshly ground black pepper
150 - 200ml vegetable or light olive oil
a little dill (finely chopped)

Garnish

baby salad leaves

Method

For The Gravadlax

Rub the vodka in to the flesh side of the salmon. Mix together the salt, sugar, spices and roughly chopped dill. Put half this mix into a plastic container. Place the salmon on top, skin-side up and cover with the rest of the mix until the salmon is buried. Cover with clingfilm and refrigerate for two to three days. Remove the salmon from the marinade and wash to remove excess salt. Dry thoroughly. Spread a thin layer of French mustard on the salmon and allow to dry briefly. Press the finely chopped dill onto the mustard-smeared salmon, until covered. Thinly slice the salmon at a 45 degree angle down to, but not including, the skin. The skin can be discarded.

> **Chef's Tip**
>
> You can cure other types of fish with this method. Halibut with a shaved apple and fennel salad is great too.

For The Cucumber Salad

Sprinkle the cucumber with a little table salt to draw out excess moisture and stand in a colander for 30 minutes.
Rinse thoroughly in cold water to remove the salt, then pat dry. To make a marinade, place the sugar, vinegar, chilli, bay leaf and star anise in a pan. Bring to a boil, then remove from the heat. Allow to cool and pass through a sieve. Combine the cucumber, marinade, shallots and chives and stir together gently so as not to break up the cucumber. Refrigerate until needed.

For The Dressing

Combine all ingredients into a food processor except the oil and dill. On a slow setting, trickle in the oil until you have a runny mayonnaise, then fold in the dill.

To Serve

Fill a small ring with marinated cucumber. Roll slices of gravadlax into a rose and place on top of the cucumber. Remove the ring. Garnish with baby salad leaves and dressing.

DUCK BREAST, SMOKED DUCK & BLACK PUDDING HOTPOT

SERVES 4

🍷 *Apollonio Salice Salentino, Puglia, 2007
(Italy)*

Ingredients

4 free range duck breasts (trimmed of sinew,
skin scored)
4 free range duck legs

Hotpot

170g black pudding (1cm diced)
50g butter
1 onion (thinly sliced)
a little thyme (picked)
4 Maris Piper (or similar) chipping potatoes
(peeled and 1cm diced)
1 ltr duck fat
duck leg spices: 10g each - cloves, cinnamon,
peppercorns and 1 star anise (dry roasted
and ground)
3 tbsp sea salt
3 tbsp caster sugar
1 orange (zest of)
natural oak chippings

Duck Jus

1 ltr duck stock
$^1/_2$ ltr real ale
Mirepoix (1 onion, 1 leek, 2 carrots, 1 stick
celery, 1 bunch thyme, all chopped)
1 tbsp caster sugar
dash Worcestershire sauce
a little olive oil

Vegetables

purple sprouting broccoli (steamed)

Method

For The Hotpot (Prepare the day before)

Mix the salt, sugar, orange zest and half tablespoon of duck spices and rub all over the duck legs. Refrigerate for 12 hours. Wash off the cure and pat dry. Line the base of a smoker or wok with tinfoil. Add oak chippings to the smoker/wok and heat over a medium heat until the chippings are smoking. Place the duck legs on a wire rack over the chippings and cover with tinfoil. Cook for 45 minutes on a very low heat. Once smoked, cook the legs in the oven at 110°C for about two hours, until tender.

Pick the meat from the bones, discarding the skin. Cook the onion gently in butter and thyme until soft but not coloured. Heat the duck fat in a pan to 130°C. Cook the potatoes in the duck fat for about five minutes, until tender and drain on a paper towel. Combine the leg meat, black pudding, onion, half the potato and a little *jus* and place in individual serving dishes. Top with the remaining potatoes.

For The Jus

Sweat the *Mirepoix* in a little olive oil. Add the beer and sugar and reduce until sticky. Add the duck stock and Worcestershire sauce and reduce until the sauce coats the back of a spoon. Pass through a fine sieve and reserve.

To Serve

Preheat oven to 180°C. Season the duck breasts and place in a cold pan, skin-side down, over a medium to high heat. Cook until the skin is crisp and golden. Place in the oven for five minutes. Remove from the oven and turn the duck breasts over so they are flesh side down and leave to rest in the pan for five minutes. Place the hotpot under the grill until the potatoes on top are crispy. Slice the duck breasts and serve on purple sprouting broccoli. Spoon the *jus* over the duck and around the plate.

> **Chef's Tip**
>
> Buy whole ducks and ask your butcher to remove the breasts and legs and keep the carcass to make stock.

BEETROOT & BLOOD ORANGE PANNA COTTA, BLOOD ORANGE, MINT & CANDIED WALNUT SALAD

SERVES 4

 Chateau de Rolland, Cru Bourgeois, Sauternes, 2004 (France)

Ingredients

Panna Cotta

500g beetroot (peeled and finely diced)
200ml double cream
100ml blood orange juice (approx 2 oranges squeezed)
100g caster sugar
4 leaves gelatine
squeeze lemon juice
4 x 5cm *dariole* moulds

Blood Orange, Mint And Candied Walnut Salad

2 blood oranges (peeled and pith removed and sliced thinly)
100g caster sugar
100g walnuts (halves)
100ml water

Mint Syrup

100g caster sugar
1/2 tbsp liquid glucose
1/2 bunch mint
icing sugar

Method

For The Panna Cotta

Blend the beetroot with a little water until a smooth purée forms. Pass through a fine sieve, squeezing the pulp to extract as much juice as possible (be careful not to push the pulp through). Gently warm 200ml of beetroot purée with the double cream, orange juice and sugar until the sugar has dissolved. Meanwhile, soak the gelatine in cold water until soft and pliable. Squeeze the gelatine to remove excess water and stir into the beetroot mixture. Add a squeeze of lemon juice to taste. Pass through a sieve again and place in a bowl set over iced water, stirring occasionally until the beetroot mix is cool and slightly thickened. Pour into *dariole* moulds and place in the fridge to set.

Chef's Tip

Make sure the panna cotta mix cools properly before pouring into the moulds. If you don't, the beetroot juice will separate.

For The Candied Walnuts

Lightly roast the walnuts and keep warm. Meanwhile, place 100g sugar, glucose and a little water in a pan and heat gently until the sugar is dissolved. Increase the heat and cook the sugar until it reaches a golden caramel. Do not stir it. Add the warm roasted walnuts to the pan and pour onto a Silpat mat (or tray with greaseproof paper). Once cool, break into small pieces.

For The Mint Syrup

Remove the leaves from the mint and boil the stalks in 100g sugar and 100ml water. Leave the syrup to cool. Chop half the mint leaves finely and add to the cool syrup.

To Serve

Dip the *dariole* moulds in a bowl of warm water until they release the panna cottas and turn out onto cold plates. Place four to five slices of orange on the plate and dust with icing sugar. Scatter over the candied walnuts and a few mint leaves. Drizzle with mint syrup.

160
THE WOOD NORTON

Worcester Road, Evesham, Worcestershire, WR11 4YB

01386 765 611
www.thewoodnorton.com

T he Vale of Evesham unfolds in its verdant magnificence near to the stunning Wood Norton hotel.

Located in the shadows of the Malvern Hills and on the northern edge of the Cotswolds, it has undergone a £4 million-plus refurbishment.

The stunning 50 bedroom hotel has an impressive history. The Grade II listed Victorian building was purchased by the exiled French Duc d'Aumale in 1872. He wanted a hunting lodge and found the scenic location most agreeable.

By 1897 he had passed the estate to his great nephew, the Duc D'Orleans, who saw Wood Norton as the ideal location to base the Bourbon-Orleans family. Around that time, the hunting lodge was converted to the hall that stands today.

The Wood Norton has played host to many notable guests from around the world. It was famously the venue for the wedding of the Princess Louise of Orleans, the grandmother to King Juan Carlos of Spain, and Prince Charles of Bourbon in 1907. It then played host to the BBC who purchased it for broadcasts outside London and in case of national emergency.

The venue is equidistant from Worcester, Stratford-upon-Avon and Cheltenham, making it the perfect location for exploring the Cotswolds, Malvern Hills and Worcestershire.

Its restaurant uses the finest vegetables, along with other stunning local produce. Guests can dine in a wood-panelled dining room, enjoy alfresco lunches on the terrace or relax in a contemporary bar.

gourmetlife

Supporting UK Producers
Providers & Diners

Relish the region's exclusive offers.
See page 003 for details.

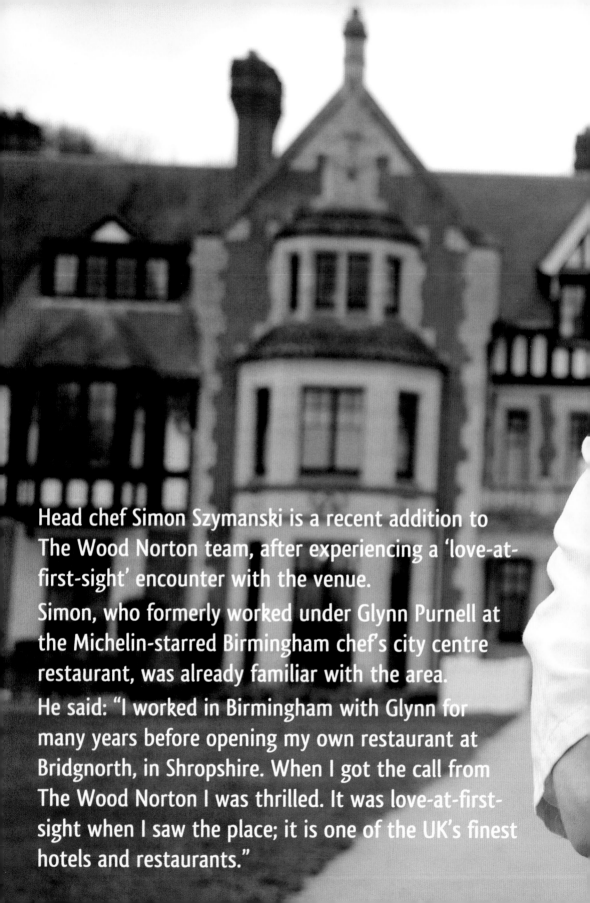

Head chef Simon Szymanski is a recent addition to The Wood Norton team, after experiencing a 'love-at-first-sight' encounter with the venue.

Simon, who formerly worked under Glynn Purnell at the Michelin-starred Birmingham chef's city centre restaurant, was already familiar with the area.

He said: "I worked in Birmingham with Glynn for many years before opening my own restaurant at Bridgnorth, in Shropshire. When I got the call from The Wood Norton I was thrilled. It was love-at-first-sight when I saw the place; it is one of the UK's finest hotels and restaurants."

SOFT BOILED DUCK EGG, SALAD OF JERSEY ROYALS & CHORIZO

SERVES 2

 Painted Wolf Roussanne 2011
(South Africa)

Ingredients

1 large duck egg
250g chorizo sausage
500g Jersey Royal potatoes
2 tbsp mayonnaise
1 packet flat leaf parsley
150ml rapeseed oil

Garnish

micro cress
parsnip crisps

Method

For The Egg

Add the duck egg into a pan of boiling water and gently simmer for six minutes. Refresh in ice cold water for ten minutes. Peel the duck egg and cut in half lengthways.

For The Jersey Royals And Chorizo

Add Jersey Royals to a pan of water, cook until tender to touch. Drain, then skin and chop into small dice.

Skin the chorizo sausage and chop into quarter-inch squares. Heat a frying pan and a little of the rapeseed oil. Brown the chorizo then remove from heat and add the remaining rapeseed oil to the frying pan to infuse the chorizo sausage.

Add the diced potato and drained chorizo into a bowl. Bind with the two tablespoons of mayonnaise and chopped parsley leaves. Season.

To Serve

Centre the potato and chorizo salad in a bowl, placing the duck egg on top with the yolk showing. Dress using the remaining infused oil on and around dish.

Chef's Tip

Duck eggs have delicious golden yolks. Spend the extra time to track down a local farm or producer who sells them directly. It's worth the extra effort.

SLOW COOKED CORNISH HAKE, LEEKS & RADISHES

SERVES 2

 Vavasour Pinot Noir 2010
(New Zealand)

Ingredients

Hake

500g Cornish hake (pin boned removed)
500ml sunflower oil
1 lemon (rind)
1 sprig thyme

Leeks And Radishes

1 bunch baby leeks
1 bunch radishes
150g salted butter

Leek Vinaigrette

2 baby leeks
salt and pepper (to season)
1 tbsp olive oil
lemon (squeeze of)

Vanilla Potatoes (Makes enough for 6)

1kg waxy new potatoes eg: Charlotte potatoes
olive oil (to cover)
1 vanilla pod

Garnish

watercress

Method

For The Leeks And Radishes

Blanch baby leeks in seasoned boiling water for two minutes. Refresh in cold water and drain.

Simmer radishes for ten minutes in salted butter and water. Remove from heat and cool.

For The Hake

Cut hake into two equal sized portions.

Add oil and infuse with lemon peel and thyme in a frying pan, on a low heat, for ten minutes. Add both pieces of hake and continue to simmer for six minutes, then remove from heat.

Lift the hake pieces from the infused oil and drain on a kitchen towel.

For The Leek Vinaigrette

Blanch the baby leeks in seasoned boiling water for two minutes, then drain. Place into a food processor, add the olive oil and blitz. Add a pinch of salt and pepper to taste and season with a touch of lemon juice.

For The Vanilla Potatoes

Wash, peel and slice the potatoes. Cover in the olive oil in a heavy bottomed pan and cook on a low heat for approximately 20 minutes. Scrape the vanilla seeds into the oil, so that the potatoes are infused with vanilla and covered in the small black seeds. Remove from the oil and drain.

To Serve

Reheat baby leeks and radishes in salted butter, using a saucepan. Add a swipe of leek vinaigrette and arrange the hake onto centre of plate.

Decorate the hake with radishes and leeks, adding a small amount of liquor from the radishes and baby leeks pan and arrange the potato slices in a line on the plate.

Chef's Tip

Establish a good relationship with your fishmonger. He'll be able to tell you how and where fish is landed. Ask about fish from day boats that is line caught and delivered overnight.

RHUBARB & CUSTARD

SERVES 2

 Gewurztraminer 2010, Vendange Manuelles, Martin Zahn, Alsace (France)

Ingredients

Rhubarb
250g rhubarb (peeled and chopped)
3 tbsp icing sugar
50g porridge oats (toasted)

Pastry Cream
250ml whole milk
40g plain flour
2 egg yolks
35g caster sugar

Sorbet
250g rhubarb (peeled and chopped)
250ml water
150g caster sugar
1 tbsp liquid glucose

Method

For The Pastry Cream
Mix the egg yolks and caster sugar together, then add flour. Bring milk to a boil, then pour onto the egg yolks, caster sugar and flour mixture. Stir until smooth. Return to heat and stir until thickened. Take off heat and allow to cool.

For The Sorbet
Boil the rhubarb, water, sugar and liquid glucose together then remove from heat. Strain, chill and freeze.

For The Rhubarb
Cook rhubarb in a saucepan with icing sugar, until tender. More icing sugar may be required if the flavour of rhubarb is too tart.

To Serve
Begin to build with alternate layers of pastry cream and rhubarb into a glass until three quarters full. Add one scoop of sorbet and finish with toasted oats.

Chef's Tip
You can add further elements to this dish to dazzle your dinner guests. Make small cubes of rhubarb jelly with the cooking liquor, or rhubarb dust, by dehydrating additional rhubarb in the oven at a very low temperature and then blitzing in a processor.

5 NORTH STREET

5 North Street, Winchcombe, Cheltenham, Gloucestershire, GL54 5LH

01242 604 566
www.5northstreetrestaurant.co.uk

Michelin starred chef Gus Ashenford worked in the nation's finest kitchens before opening the award-winning 5 North Street, in Winchcombe.

He started his career in 1986 at catering college in Cheltenham, where he met his wife-to-be, Kate, who was in the same class.

His first professional cheffing job was at Calcot Manor in Tetbury, where he worked under Ramon Farthing. Soon after, he landed a post at the three starred Waterside Inn at Bray-on-Thames, where he worked with the Roux brothers for four years as chef de partie.

Gus then went to Lovells at Windrush Farm, where he became head chef at the age of 24 and achieved a Michelin star within 18 months.

A head chef position, at Chavignol in Chipping Norton, followed and Gus again earned a Michelin star within a year.

He next moved to Chavignol at the Old Mill, in Shipston On Stour, before he and wife Kate launched 5 North Street in January 2003. They achieved their Michelin star a year later and have kept it since then.

Gus said, "Kate and I had worked in numerous exceptional restaurants, but we found a lot of inspiration when we went to Shaun Hill's Merchant House, in Ludlow. The restaurant was stripped back - there were no table cloths - it was simply great food and great service."

Kate added, "When we opened the restaurant, we decided we wanted to let the food and service do all the talking."

This recipe has ensured a full house ever since.

Relish the region's exclusive offers.
See page 003 for details.

MANGO RIPPLE ICE CREAM WITH GOLDEN RAISIN PUREE & GINGER SNAP

SERVES 4

 Late Noble Riesling, by Paul Clever
(South Africa)

Ingredients

Mango Ripple

1 mango
25g sugar
1 dsp glucose

Ice Cream

285ml double cream
285ml milk
2 vanilla pods
8 duck egg yolks
50g caster sugar
1 small ladle glucose

Golden Raisin Purée

250g golden raisins
25g caster sugar
50ml apple juice
50ml sweet wine
1 dsp sherry vinegar

Ginger Snap

50g butter
30g demerara sugar
75g golden syrup
100g plain flour
3g bicarbonate of soda
5g ground ginger

Garnish

1 mango
baby basil leaves

Method

For The Ice Cream

Boil and infuse cream, milk and vanilla. Using a food processor, whisk yolks and sugar until white. Pour liquid onto the yolk mixture. Cook to 75°C and then pass through a *chinois*. Whisk by hand until cool then add glucose. When cool, churn in an ice cream machine.

For The Mango Ripple

Peel, de-stone and chop the mango. Gently boil with the sugar and glucose. Liquidise and pass through a sieve. Allow to cool. Stir into the ice cream at the final stage to give a ripple effect. Save a little mango syrup to poach the mango balls.

For The Ginger Snap

Cream butter, sugar and syrup in a food processor. Fold in the flour, bicarbonate of soda and ginger. Leave the paste to rest. Roll out onto a sheet, then cut biscuits into 15cm long by 1.5cm wide rectangles. Rest again. Bake for seven to eight minutes at 180°C until golden brown - include all of the trimmings. When cooked, rest on a cooling wire. Grind the cooked trimmings with the end of a rolling pin to make a powder. Reserve for later to sit the ice cream on.

For The Golden Raisin Purée

Gently reduce the raisins, wine, sugar and juice. Remove half of the raisins for garnish. Liquidise the remaining raisins into a purée. Do not pass through a sieve.

For The Garnish

Peel the mango. Use a Parisienne scoop to take small balls of flesh from the fruit. Poach for two to three minutes in the mango syrup.

To Serve

Assemble as pictured and decorate with baby basil leaves.

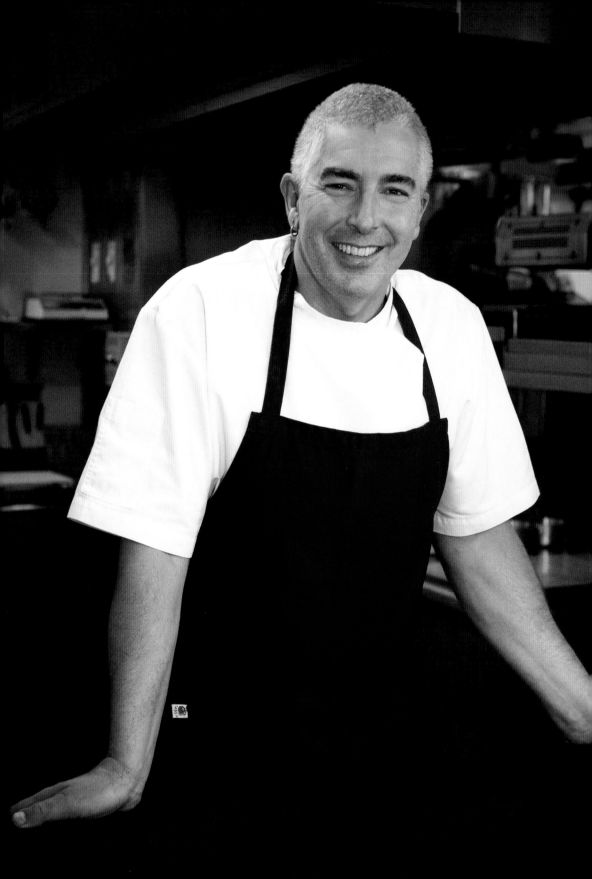

175
RELISH COTSWOLDS & OXFORDSHIRE LARDER

INTRODUCTION BY DAVID EVERITT-MATTHIAS

David Everitt-Matthias is one of Britain's greatest chefs. He has been running Le Champignon Sauvage with his wife Helen since 1987 and has famously never missed a service. In that time they have been quietly amassing a range of accolades including two Michelin stars, two stars from the Harden's Guide and four AA rosettes.

The way I look at things is simple. I have my very own pantry in my big back yard of Gloucestershire and the Cotswolds. It's a remarkable place. I don't think there's anywhere else in the UK that is quite so good.

We're blessed to be surrounded by great producers and great natural ingredients. That means we can put the best seasonal flavours on the plate. A lot of local chefs are in the same position. There are some great restaurants out there - places like 5 North Street spring to mind - where local flavours are showcased.

I came up from London and I think this region is fantastic. My wife and I visit Normandy quite a bit and there are a great number of similarities between the Cotswolds and that region of France. Both areas have great dairies and creameries and their food is highly influenced by butter and cream.

At Le Champignon Sauvage, we love natural ingredients. I tend to forage once a week, though most of my foraging is inspired by my wife. She goes running with our dogs nearby and whilst running, she'll spy wild ingredients that we can go and harvest later.

Spring and Autumn time are both phenomenal. We get all sorts of produce. There are acorns and crab apples in Autumn and Jack-by-the-Hedge in spring. The ingredients available to us change throughout the seasons. It's not all about foraging, of course. We are blessed in having good contacts with many of our local suppliers.

Hamish Campbell, for instance, supplies our oil. He brings in high quality rapeseed oil. It has a uniquely nutty flavour and a wonderfully deep golden colour. I remember him coming into the restaurant many, many years ago. He offered me a bottle of oil and I loved it. He didn't know of our reputation but was later pleasantly surprised and delighted that I wanted to promote his oil.

In Spring, we have Evesham asparagus. I'm convinced that it's the best in the world. It is phenomenal. It's very sweet and succulent, so very little needs doing to it. When the first bunches come through in Spring, we put it in the pan and dry roast it, then we add a little butter at the end. We don't even steam it. Cooking it that way serves to re-emphasise the sweetness.

There's a wonderful selection of cheeses within the area. I'm a huge fan of St Eadburgha, from Broadway, as well as the Cerney Pyramid, which is from Cirencester. Then there's Stinking Bishop, from Charles Martell. We also get organic milk from Jess's Ladies Organic Farm Milk, in Hardwicke. It's a delicious product, it's a bit like Gold Top. They do a breakfast milk, which is wonderfully creamy. It's perfect for use in ice creams - it's very, very creamy.

We have a number of great producers of beer in the area, too. One of my favourites is a Porter beer, from Battledown Brewery, which is fairly dark and has mild hints of coffee flavour - it's perfect for use in chocolate and caramel desserts.

One of the joys of being based in this area is that there's been an increase in the number of small producers in recent times. It's almost going back to the way things used to be, many years ago, with plenty of micro producers and lots of farmers markets. We're very fortunate to be in this part of the world. We have great produce and great producers right on our doorstep. Its a delight to be able to champion some of our favourite producers, suppliers and chefs in this prestigious cookbook.

Charlie Beldam

COTSWOLD GOLD

Cotswold Gold Ltd, East Lodge Farm, Stanton, Broadway, Worcestershire, WR12 7NH
T: 07867 938 221
www.cotswoldgold.co.uk

Founded by Charlie Beldam in 2010 after graduating from the Royal Agricultural College, Cirencester. Charlie's ambition was to develop a British alternative to olive oil that would be both healthy and sustainable. The company produces extra virgin, cold-pressed rapeseed oil using grain grown on Charlie's family farm in Gloucestershire. The oil is extracted using traditional cold-pressing methods that preserve the nutritional content of the grain to create a delicately flavoured, vibrantly coloured oil.

Cotswold Gold can be used for all cooking needs, from salad dressings and dips through to high temperature frying, making it the most versatile oil on the market. A staple in many restaurants and the kitchens of top chefs including Raymond Blanc, Martin Blunos, James Martin and Dave Watts to name a few.

DAYLESFORD ORGANIC FARMSHOP & CAFE
Daylesford near Kingham, Gloucestershire, GL56 0YG
T: 01608 731 700
www.daylesfordorganic.com

The ultimate farm shop, café restaurant and cookery school. All meat and poultry, fruit and vegetables are from their market garden; bread from their bakery; cheese, milk and yoghurt from their creamery. Daylesford also offer cookery courses and demos with their in-house chefs.

MERE FISH FARM

Mere Fish Farm, Ivymead, Mere, Warminster
Wiltshire, BA12 6EN
www.merefishfarm.co.uk

*Established 1982 'family run' trout farm and smokery.
Fish reared in spring water. Quality fresh and
smoked trout products. They supply chef Ron of
Ronnie's Of Thornbury amongst others in the region.
Countrywide delivery.*

UPTON WINES

8 New Street, Upton-upon-Severn, Worcester
Worcestershire, WR8 0HR
T: 01684 592 668
www.uptonwines.co.uk

*Upton Upon Severn Wines is a family run business, supplying
the region's favourite restaurants for more than 20 years.*

*Specialist wines are supplied by father and son team, Alan
and Andy Goadby, from their shop in Upton-upon-Severn.*

*Many wines selected to match recipes in this book are by
wine writer Philippe Boucheron www.pboucheron.com*

HALEN MÔN SALT

The Anglesey Sea Salt Company Ltd, Brynsiencyn
Isle of Anglesey, LL61 6TQ, Wales
T: 01248 430 871
www.halenmon.com

*From humble beginnings on the family kitchen Aga,
boiling sea water which surrounds them, to being
enjoyed around the world by chefs, food lovers and
even the odd US President. Purported to be the purest
sea salt, from the Menai Strait.*

HERITAGE SILVERWARE LTD

Heritage Collection™, 62 Green Lane, Small Heath
Birmingham, West Midlands, B9 5DB
T: 0121 7730 724
www.heritage-silverware.com

*Heritage Collection is a leading manufacturer of bespoke
tableware for discerning hotels and restaurants around the
world. Based in Birmingham, the company was formed in
1976 as Heritage Silverware Ltd. From silver plated
afternoon tea stands, stainless steel or silver plated cutlery
to wine trolleys, the unique designs created by the family's
years of experience, give dining the edge.*

REVILLS FARM SHOP

Bourne Road, Defford, Worcestershire WR8 9BS

T: 01386 750 466

www.revillsfarmshop.co.uk

Family run Revills was started in 2003 by Isabel Revill. She began selling the fresh asparagus tips they grew in the field next to the barn. They are now both growers and suppliers of of 'The best asparagus in the world' (chef David Everitt-Matthias of two Michelin star Le Champignon Sauvage, Cheltenham), as well as sourcing fine quality produce from around the UK for their tranquil farm shop and café near Pershore. Dedicated to good quality, great tasting food.

JUST OIL

Just Oil Ltd, Wade Lane Farm, Hill Ridware

Staffordshire, WS15 3RE.

T: 01543 493 081

www.justoil.co.uk

Family farmed rapeseed oil located in Staffordshire for four generations. Supplying restaurants and retail outlets across the heart of England with their award-winning range of Just Cold Pressed Rapeseed Oil products which now includes 'Just Crisps' using rapeseed oil to cook them. Grown, harvested, cold pressed, filtered and bottled on their farm.

SHIPTON MILL LTD

Long Newnton, Tetbury, Gloucestershire, GL8 8RP

T: 01666 505 050

www.shipton-mill.com

Set in a beautiful Cotswold valley near Tetbury, the mill at Shipton Moyne Wood has been producing flour since the time of the Domesday Book. Today it produces a wide variety of speciality flours, using both traditional grain and traditional methods, and they supply many of the region's restaurants. They have also developed speciality flours with chef Raymond Blanc of Le Manoir and are also the owners of Bibury Court Hotel, Bibury, Gloucestershire.

BROCK HALL FARM DAIRY GOATS CHEESES

Chelmarsh, Bridgnorth, Shropshire, WV16 6QA.

01746 862 533

www.brockhallfarm.com

Sarah Hampton is as passionate about her produce as they come. Over the years, she has lovingly built up a herd of pedigree Saanen goats, whose superb milk is skilfully used to create a range of unique and wonderful artisan cheeses.

Through attention to detail and commitment to quality, Sarah has developed a range of award-winning goat's cheeses, suitable for culinary uses and for the cheeseboard. In 2012 her Capra Nouveau, a semi-soft washed-rind cheese, was awarded three Great Taste gold stars and was named as a Top 50 Food in Great Britain.

Sarah and her small team are proud to supply Le Champignon Sauvage and other prestigious establishments in the heart of England and beyond.

R-OIL

Swell Buildings Farm, Lower Swell, Stow on the Wold, Gloucestershire, GL54 1HG
T: 01451 870 387
www.r-oil.co.uk

Hamish's family have been farming at Swell Buildings Farm since 1988 but only began experimenting with production of their own cold-pressed rapeseed oil in 2005, having previously used rapeseed as a 'break crop' to help improve the yield of following cereal crops. Supported by friends, family and local chefs giving feedback, by November 2005 they believed they had the perfect product. Now they supply some of the finest chefs in the region. Grown on the free draining Cotswold soils gives it a unique flavour when it comes to cold-pressed rapeseed oils.

"Hamish's rapeseed oil offers a uniquely nutty flavour and a wonderfully deep golden colour" Two star Michelin chef, David Everitt Mathias, Le Champignon Sauvage, Cheltenham.

AUBREY ALLEN DIRECT
108 Warwick Street, Leamington, Warwickshire, CV32 4QP.
T: 01926 311 208
www.aubreyallen.co.uk

Aubrey Allen have been serving the Warwickshire public the finest meat since 1933. They carefully select and inspect all of their suppliers and can trace their meat from farm to plate. They are renowned for meat such as granite grassland reared Cornish lamb, corn fed Loire Valley hens, and free range pork produced by 'Pig Farmer of the Year' Jimmy Butler.

HAYMANS FISHERIES
21-23 The Covered Market, Oxford, OX1 3DU
T: 01865 726 944
www.haymansfisheries.co.uk

Haymans Fisheries offers high quality, fresh fish and seafood through their fishmonger shops and direct to the catering industry. Fish is sourced daily from inshore boats around the coast to ensure freshness and continuity of supply.

Ron Faulkner, Ronnie's Of Thornbury

Dave Watts, The Star Inn

5 NORTH STREET
5 North Street, Winchcombe, Cheltenham,
Gloucestershire, GL54 5LH
T: 01242 604 566
www.5northstreetrestaurant.co.uk

ARROW MILL HOTEL
Arrow, Near Alcester, Warwickshire, B49 5NL
T: 01789 762 419
www.arrowmill.com

BIBURY COURT
Bibury, Cirencester, Gloucestershire, GL7 5NT
T: 01285 740 337
www.biburycourt.com

BUCKLAND MANOR
Buckland, Gloucestershire, WR12 7LY
T: 01386 852 626
www.bucklandmanor.co.uk

THE DINING ROOM & COTSWOLD GRILL
Cotswold House Hotel and Spa, The Square, Chipping Campden,
Gloucestershire, GL55 6AN
T: 01386 840 330
www.cotswoldhouse.com

ECKINGTON MANOR
Hammock Road, Eckington, Worcestershire, WR10 3BJ
T: 01386 751 600
www.eckingtonmanor.co.uk

ELLENBOROUGH PARK
Southam Road, Cheltenham, Gloucestershire, GL52 3NJ
T: 01242 545 454
www.ellenboroughpark.com

THE FEATHERED NEST COUNTRY INN
Nether Westcote, Oxfordshire, OX7 6SD
T: 01993 833 030
www.thefeatherednestinn.co.uk

Kuba Winkowski, The Feathered Nest Country Inn

Mark Chandler, The White Hart

THE KING'S HEAD INN
The Green, Bledington, Oxfordshire, OX7 6XQ
T: 01608 658 365
www.thekingsheadinn.net

LE MANOIR AUX QUAT'SAISONS
Church Road, Great Milton, Oxford, OX44 7PD
T: 0184 427 8881
www.manoir.com

LOWER SLAUGHTER MANOR
Lower Slaughter, Gloucestershire, GL54 2HP
T: 01451 820 456
www.lowerslaughter.co.uk

THE NUT TREE INN
Main Street, Murcott, Oxon, OX5 2RE
T: 01865 331 253
www.nuttreeinn.co.uk

RONNIE'S OF THORNBURY
11 St Mary Street, Thornbury, South Gloucestershire, BS35 2AB
T: 01454 411 137
www.ronnies-restaurant.co.uk

THE SWAN INN
Swinbrook, Near Burford, Oxon, OX18 4DY
T: 01993 823 339
www.theswanswinbrook.co.uk

THE STAR INN
Watery Lane, Sparsholt, Wantage, Oxfordshire, OX12 9PL
T: 01235 751 873
www.thestarsparsholt.co.uk

THE WHITE HART
Main Road, Fyfield, Abingdon, Oxon, OX13 5LW
T: 01865 390 585
www.whitehart-fyfield.com

THE WOOD NORTON
Worcester Road, Evesham, Worcestershire, WR11 4YB
T: 01386 765 611
www.thewoodnorton.com

Great Club, Great Food, Join Now...
Exclusive Lifestyle Dining Club for the Heart of England

- Accepted across the region with exclusive added value and offers from the finest restaurants, hotels, cookery schools and suppliers in the Heart of England
- Membership entitles you to discounts off locally sourced menus at some of the finest venues, including Michelin accredited restaurants
- Savings at delis, farm shops and cookery schools

- Added value offers on special menus, afternoon teas and overnight breaks - saving from 20% off dining to 50% off dine and stay accommodation packages
- Supporters of the region's producers, providers and diners.

Relish the Heart of England's exclusive offers

Special Offer

Join *gourmetlife* - Lifestyle Dining Club, for half price when you mention '**Relish**'.
Visit www.gourmet-life.co.uk/halfprice and follow the instructions. All new members are entered into a monthly draw to win a Michelin star meal for two!

www.twitter.com/gourmet_life
www.Facebook.com/MichelinDinersMidlands

For a list of participating venues visit
www.gourmet-life.co.uk

Relish PUBLICATIONS

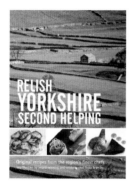

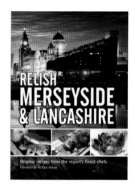

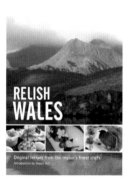
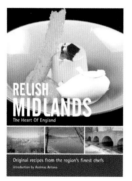

BEST OF BRITISH

Relish Publications is an independent publishing house offering an exclusive insight to Britain's finest restaurants and chefs with their series of award-winning recipe books.

Each book contains signature recipes from your favourite chefs, recommended wines, stunning food photography and an impressive guide to each participating restaurant, plus a larder featuring the region's best produce suppliers. These ingredients make the Relish series an ultimate 'foodies' guide for individuals wishing to dine in great restaurants or create outstanding recipes at home.

The series of beautiful hard back recipe books are available to buy in the featured restaurants, all good bookshops and online at the Relish bookshop or Amazon.

For more information please visit **www.relishpublications.co.uk**

LOOKING TO DINE IN THE UK'S FINEST RESTAURANTS?

Visit the Relish Restaurant Guide to find the very best your region has to offer.

The Relish team has worked with all of the chefs listed on the Relish website and have visited every highly recommended and acclaimed restaurant. This recipe makes the **Relish Restaurant Guide** genuine and unique.

If you would like to be taken on an epic journey to the finest restaurants in each region, to download more mouth-watering recipes, to join our exclusive Relish Rewards club, or to add to your collection of Relish books, visit **www.relishpublications.co.uk**

WHAT'S APP-ENING?

Our series of regional cookbooks are now available to download and purchase.

Browse hundreds of recipes with beautiful photography and easy to follow instructions from a selection of the UK's finest chefs and restaurants.

 Download your FREE sample pages now on the App Store/Relish Cookbook.

Apple, the Apple logo and iPhone are trademarks of Apple Inc, registered in the US and other countries, App Store is a service mark of Apple Inc.

Relish PUBLICATIONS

Duncan and Teresa Peters founded Relish Publications in 2009, through a passion for good food, a love of publishing and recognising the need to promote the fantastic chefs and restaurants each region in the UK has to offer.

Since launching, their goal was simple. Create beautiful books with high quality contributors (each edition features a selection of the region's top chefs) to build a unique and invaluable recipe book.

As recipe book specialists, their team work with hundreds of chefs personally to ensure each edition exceeds the readers' expectations.

Thank you for Relishing with us!

HERE'S WHAT SOME OF BRITAIN'S BEST CHEFS HAVE SAID ABOUT WORKING WITH RELISH

"The Relish cookbook offers the home cook some great inspiration to make the most of these wonderful ingredients in season." *Tom Kitchin, The Kitchin, Edinburgh*

"Relish Publications are always very impressive books, beautifully assembled, with fabulous images and a real pleasure to absorb." *Geoffrey Smeddle, The Peat Inn, St Andrews*

"Relish Wales is a fabulous way to showcase some of our beautiful country's fabulous eateries and to be able to share our food with a wider audience." *Stephen Terry, The Hardwick, Wales*

"I'm immensely proud to be writing the foreword to a book that celebrates the best of Midland's food." *Andreas Antona, Simpsons Restaurant, Birmingham*

GLOSSARY

ACIDULATED WATER
When an acid is added to water - lemon juice, lime juice, or vinegar. This prevents skinned fruits or vegetables from browning.

BAIN-MARIE
A pan or other container of hot water with a bowl placed on top of it. This allows the steam from the water to heat the bowl so ingredients can be gently heated or melted in the bowl.

BEURRE BLANC
French translates as 'white butter'. A hot emulsified butter sauce made with a reduction of vinegar and/or white wine (normally Muscadet) and grey shallots. Cold, whole butter is blended off the heat to prevent separation.

BLANCH
Boiling an ingredient before removing it and plunging it in ice cold water in order to stop the cooking process.

CHINOIS
A conical sieve with an extremely fine mesh. It is used to strain custards, purées, soups and sauces, producing a very smooth texture.

CLARIFIED BUTTER
Milk fat rendered from butter to separate the milk solids and water from the butter fat.

COMPOTE
French for 'mixture'. Whole fruits are cooked in water with sugar and spices. The syrup may be seasoned and can be served either warm or cold.

CONFIT
A method of cooking where the meat is cooked and submerged in a liquid to add flavour. Often this liquid is rendered fat. Confit can also apply to fruits - fruit confits are cooked and preserved in sugar, the result is like candied fruits.

DARIOLE
A French term that refers to small, cylinder shaped moulds.

DEGLAZE
A fancy term for using the flavour-packed brown bits stuck to the bottom of a pan to make a pan sauce or gravy.

EMULSION/EMULSIFY
In the culinary arts, an emulsion is a mixture of two liquids that would ordinarily not mix together, like oil and vinegar.

FRENCH TRIM
A method of preparing a rack of lamb by cutting the fat out around each bone down to the meat and scraping the bones of all sinew and fat. Then the lamb is cut between the bones and through the eye of the lamb, leaving 1cm of meat still attached at the bottom.

JULIENNE
A culinary knife cut in which the food item is cut into long thin strips, similar to matchsticks.

JUS
The natural juices given off by the food. To prepare a natural jus, the cook may simply skim off the fat from the juices left after cooking and bring the remaining meat stock and water to a boil.

MIREPOIX
Combination of celery (pascal, celery or celeriac), onions and carrots. There are many regional mirepoix variations, which can sometimes be just one of these ingredients, or include additional spices.

MONTE
Sauce finishing. Adding small quantities of butter (emulsify) to thicken a sauce.

PANE
To coat with flour, beaten egg and breadcrumbs.

PASTEURISE
A process of heating a food, which is usually a liquid, to a specific temperature for a period of time, sufficient to destroy certain microorganisms.

REDUCTION
The process of thickening a liquid in order to intensify the flavour. This is done by evaporating the moisture in a liquid.

SABAYON
Made by beating egg yolks with a liquid over simmering water until thickened and increased in volume. The liquid can be water, but Champagne or wine is often used.